# Help! My Toddler Is Not Eating.

## A 30-Day Plan to Get Your Picky Eater to Enjoy New Food.

ISBN: 978-1-9163833-0-2

First published in 2020

## Disclaimer

## Contents

Introduction 7

Day 1: Just How Picky is My Child? 13

Day 2: Your Own Food History 19

Day 3: Children Are Good at Growing! 24

Day 4: Do Children Need to Eat Differently from Their Parents? 30

Day 5: What Children Need to Eat 36

Day 6: Mealtime Routines 46

Day 7: Milk, Juice and Yoghurt 52

Day 8: Vitamins & Minerals 60

Day 9: Iron & Iron Deficiency Anaemia 72

Day 10: Our Natural Food Preferences 80

Day 11: Learning to Like 90

Day 12: Food Neophobia 98

Day 13: Exposure 104

Day 14: Repeated Exposure 113

Day 15: Pressure to Eat 120

Day 16: Reducing Mealtime Anxiety 130

Day 17: Children with Food-Related Anxiety or Phobia 136

Day 18: Oral sensitivity 142

Day 19: Boundaries and Routines 149

Day 20: Don't Offer Alternatives 156

Day 21: Ignoring Unwanted Behaviour 161

Day 22: Giving Effective Praise 176

Day 23: Treats and Bribes 181

Day 24: Role Modelling 188

Day 25: Giving Your Child Some Control 200

Day 26: Portion Sizes 209

Day 27: Food Chaining 218

Day 28: Children with Special Dietary Needs 230

Day 29: Reflux and Constipation 247

Day 30: Keep Going 251

About the Author 264

Appendix: Fortifying your child's diet 268

# Introduction

Feeding young children can be stressful. This applies to both new parents and those with more experience. It can even apply to grandparents.

Providing nourishment to a child is one of a parent's most basic responsibilities[1] and we feel that pressure acutely.

When children refuse food, their parents experience all sorts of emotions and reactions. Parents of children who have feeding problems experience emotional distress and a lot more parenting stress than parents of children who do not[2]. Although the distress can be incredibly frustrating, many of these fears and feelings are rooted in a deep evolutionary need to nurture our children.

Being a parent is said to be one of the hardest jobs in the world. Mealtimes are a prime demonstration of that difficulty.

There is the practical, day-to-day responsibility of sourcing and preparing meals. Then there are the social and personal pressures to provide healthy meals and snacks.

On top of this, for many parents, there is the anxiety and frustration of managing a toddler who will simply *not eat* the healthy food you have gone to such an effort to prepare.

## You are not alone

Picky eating and other eating problems are incredibly common.

- One study in the US followed 120 children from when they were 2 until they were 11 years old. Between 13% and 22% of the children were reported to be picky eaters[3]. Although the picky eating improved over time, 40% of the children were picky eaters for more than two years.
- Another research team in Quebec, Canada, assessed 1,498 children three times between the ages of 2 ½ to 4 years. Some 30% were picky eaters at some point during the study[4].

- In the UK, researchers studying all babies born in the former Avon Health Authority area between April 1991 and December 1992 (7,420 children in total) showed an incidence of picky eating of between 9.7% and 14.7%[5].
- More recently in Norway, 26% of the 795 children studied were picky with food at 4 years old *and* when they were followed up two years later[6].

## Nutrition issues

Picky eaters have been shown to have a lower intake of vitamins and minerals[7].

Iron and zinc intakes, in particular, are likely to be low if your child is a picky eater[8]. This is unsurprising, as picky eaters have also been shown to have a lower intake of foods rich in vitamins and minerals, such as meat, fish, vegetables and whole grains[9].

Both iron and zinc are important for appetite[10]. Poor intake of iron and zinc have both been associated with behavioural problems in young children[11].

Where picky eating persists until children are aged 7 ½, zinc intakes are even lower, with a full 69% of children taking less zinc than the lower end of recommended[12].

On Day 8 of this programme, I will look specifically at vitamins and minerals.

## Long-term problems

If not managed early on, picky eating can lead to problems later in life.

Researchers have discovered that picky eating in childhood correlates with picky eating in adolescence[13] and as an adult[14]. The longer a child is a picky eater, the greater the chance that he will be a picky eater as a young adult[15].

Other researchers have discovered that the range of foods a child will try aged 4 is a good predictor of which foods he will try when an adult[16].

All of this means that, if not treated early on, children who are picky eaters often remain picky eaters into their teens, with all the nutritional problems that come with it.

More dangerously, picky eating is also linked with eating disorders. One study interviewed over 800 families three times as the children were growing up: once when the children were aged between 1-10 years, again when they were 9-18 years old and again between the ages of 11-21. The study found that picky eating was a risk factor for developing anorexia nervosa in adolescence[17].

A German study of 426 children aged 8 to 12 found that picky eaters were more likely to exhibit problem behaviours than non-picky eaters[18].

You may be all too familiar with the problems that picky eating can cause – and really don't need me to make you even more worried about your child's eating habits.

You will already be very familiar with the tantrums at mealtimes, the struggles over feeding and the special meals that you have prepared that research tells us parents go through[19]. You may even have sought help through your child's GP, Paediatrician or Health Visitor.

You may feel blamed, which parents often do[20].

Lots of parents will have been told that this is just a normal developmental stage and that your child will grow out of it. For many children, this may be the case. For others, problems can become ingrained and persist into adolescence and adulthood. The nutritional deficiencies that follow can perpetuate behavioural problems.

In any case, tackling picky eating can prevent many frustrating mealtimes and hours of worry for parents. It's worth doing.

## How to use this book

I recommend that you work through the chapters of the book in order, day by day.

Because I know that many parents will nevertheless want to skip straight to the bits that seem most relevant to them, I sometimes repeat important points from an earlier chapter, just in case readers have skipped ahead. Do let me know whether this works for you so I can tweak it in later editions if needs be. You can contact me either through my website (*fussyaboutfood.com*), through my Facebook page (Dr Elizabeth Roberts: *facebook.com/drelizabethroberts*) or by emailing me direct (*elizabeth@fussyaboutfood.com*).

You might want to read and practice one chapter every day, reaching the end of the book after 30 days. Some chapters might be less relevant to you and you might read through these and go straight on to the next chapter, finishing before the 30 days are up.

On the other hand, you might find that you need to practice one of the chapters for more than one day, or that you just need to pause occasionally. Your 30 days might, therefore, take you two or three months. Do whatever feels right – just don't go too fast and skip the practices! If you would like more free copies of the worksheets that you can print out, then head over to *fussyaboutfood.com/worksheets*. If you are prompted for a code, then enter *BOOK20*.

The first part of the book describes the nutritional aspects of fussy or picky eating because my experience has taught me that parents worry about this the most. The second part, the psychology of how we learn to eat (and how we can influence this), is perhaps even more important – it is the chicken of the problem, so to speak. The nutritional consequences are the egg.

## Note on style

I use 'he' and 'she' interchangeably throughout the book. This is not to imply that any specific section is more relevant to boys or to girls, it's just for literary style and to balance the sexes.

## And now...

...It's over to you. The information within this book has helped many families already. I hope it helps your family, too. Your journey to getting your picky eater to enjoy new foods starts here.

# Day 1: Just How Picky is My Child?

The first question to answer seems simple, but it could be deceptive: how picky *is* my child?

To answer the question, we need to understand what is meant by picky eating, as different people will have different ideas about what constitutes "picky".

For example, researchers at the University of Minnesota in Minneapolis interviewed 88 parents about meals at home and how their children ate[1]. In these interviews, parents defined fussy or picky eating in different ways.

Some parents said their child was a picky eater if she didn't like a few foods. Others said that their child was picky only if she had a very limited range of acceptable foods. Some parents identified their child as being picky if she was put off by the texture or appearance of certain foods. Yet other parents defined picky eating as their child being fearful or apprehensive of new foods.

As you can see, picky eating to one parent might be very different from picky eating for another parent. So, for the duration of this book, let's make sure we're on the same page.

We can divide picky, fussy and selective eating into several different categories, which depend on the nature and severity of the problem.

The definitions we'll borrow for this purpose come from physical medicine, psychiatry, and psychology/behavioural research.

- **Picky or fussy eating**
  Part of normal child development. A child is expected to grow out of this issue.
- **Selective eating**
  Often associated with older children who have not grown out of the picky or fussy eating stage[2]. It is characterised by having strong likes and dislikes, eating a limited variety of foods, being reluctant to try new

foods and liking meals prepared in a certain way.

- **Avoidant/restrictive food intake disorder (ARFID)**[3]
  Where a child avoids food to the extent that they are not able to take adequate nutrition from their diet; leading to weight loss, poor growth or nutritional deficiencies. Children experiencing ARFID often need specialist input.

- **Food neophobia**
  Being reluctant to try new and unfamiliar foods[4]. As I explain on Day 12, neophobia is also part of a child's normal development.

## Why is my child a picky eater?

That's another question with many possible answers!

There are some genetic, developmental and medical reasons why one child is pickier or more selective with their eating than another child. For some children, selective eating may be linked to other symptoms of anxiety, mood or attention-deficit/ hyperactivity disorder[5] (ADD/ ADHD). Other children may have sensory processing issues or struggle more with adapting to change and new experiences.

While medical reasons may impact some children's diet, it is also true that a child's dietary intake can be expanded regardless of the reason for the restriction. Poor intake of the various nutrients needed for good health can affect behaviour[6], which might make new experiences even more difficult for a child to cope with. It's a vicious cycle.

### Natural preferences

I meet many parents who tell me that their child will only eat bland food, or will only eat KFC chicken nuggets, never homemade chicken nuggets. They often assume that something must be wrong with their child to be like this. For this reason, I think it is helpful to start by understanding some of our "normal" food preferences.

Human beings prefer sweet foods and fatty foods. This is probably because sweet foods are good sources of calories, needed for energy. Calories weren't always so easy to come by! The jury is out on salty foods, but we are probably naturally inclined to like these too. This might be because salt, in small amounts, is essential to our diet. We have to *learn* to like bitter and, to a lesser degree, sour tastes.

We naturally enjoy crunchy textures, but also foods that are soft and easy to eat. From an evolutionary perspective, crunchy usually means fresh, while mushy and easily guzzled means we can get lots of calories in quickly, with minimal effort. Human evolution tends to prefer ways of consuming calories as easily and copiously as possible. If you think about it, many of our quick-and-easy foods are sloppy in texture and seem to slide down. One of the common complaints I hear from people trying to eat more healthily is "it takes so long to chew everything"!

Children are no exception to these natural preferences. They might take a little while to get used to some textures, like sloppier foods, or chewy meat. Apart from this, they like sweet things, just like adults do.

## Minds still maturing

The difference between a child and most adults is that we have the ability to reflect on whether a food or meal is healthy or not (at least most of the time). Although this does not always mean that we make the healthiest choice, we are at least *aware* when one food is less healthy than another.

Young children have no such concept. They may be able to mimic the words you have used to describe one food over another, 'healthy' or 'unhealthy', but they have no real understanding of what this means. The concept of 'healthy' is just too abstract for them to process yet, and it will be a few years before they can do it. This means that they are rarely going to choose a food with an acquired taste, or that needs more work to chew, over a food that is instantly palatable, likeable and familiar.

## Manufacturer manipulation

Food manufacturers spend millions researching just the right amount of sugar, salt, and fat to make a food optimally palatable. They also study other food qualities, like "mouthfeel" and texture.

For instance, many savoury snack foods contain a compound called maltodextrin. While maltodextrin has no taste to humans, it fires up the reward centre in our brains in the same way as sugar (or sweet taste) does[7]. Once you pop, you really can't stop.

***

I mention all this so that you might understand why it is perfectly natural for young children, guided by taste and human instincts alone, to prefer the uniformly processed frozen chicken nuggets to the ones that you have so lovingly made.

Natural preferences aside, children can and do learn to like many different textures and complex flavour combinations. By acting now, you are offering your child the best possibility of widening their dietary intake and providing the best possible nutrition.

We know that behavioural strategies can improve a child's picky eating[8]. The strategies used in this book have all been proven to be effective at managing picky eating.

A note on language: although I sometimes refer to picky or fussy eating in this book, I think it important to not use this language with your child. Children will often grow into the labels that we give them and meet our expectations – good and bad. I still remember one young boy, taking part in a healthy family food programme that I ran in Wales, who declared: "I won't eat that! I'm a fussy eater!"

## Day 1: Try this at home

One test that experts use to determine how picky or fussy a child is in research projects is called the Child Eating Behaviour Questionnaire (CEBQ)[9].

The first day of your journey towards getting your picky toddler to eat new foods starts with completing an adapted version of this questionnaire. I will ask you to complete this questionnaire again halfway through this book, and again at the end of the programme.

You can complete the questionnaire online at *www.fussyaboutfood.com/survey*. If prompted to enter a code, please use *BOOK20*.

If you complete the questionnaire three times, then I can send you the results for all three. By completing the questionnaire three times you will be able to see just how much progress you and your child have made – and how some of the challenging exercises have paid off.

# Day 2: Your Own Food History

As new parents, we begin with the best intentions for feeding our child. We carefully plan the weaning process – cooking and freezing weaning foods in advance, planning out the stages and reading at least one book on the topic. We promise never to use pre-packaged food, to always cook from scratch and to never bribe our children with edible treats.

But then life takes over. We're busy, one or more additions to the family come along, and many of our intentions tumble away. This is when we often fall back on habits from our own childhood. Without consciously considering it, we apply the same rules to our children that we grew up with.

Sometimes this works the other way around. We vow to never impose the rules and habits we had to abide by onto our own children. Much of my own interest in nutrition came from switching households aged ten – from the healthy eating habits of my mother's house (and her constant diets – not so good) to the less healthy and less restrictive eating habits of my father's house.

Some of you reading this will instantly think of childhood food habits that you swore you would never repeat with your own children.

For example, you may have been made to finish your plate. Now you are still unable to stop eating until your plate is cleared, even if you are full. You may have been made to sit at the table until everybody was finished and can remember to this day the excruciating minutes of boredom that seemed to stretch out for hours. You promised it would be different for your own children, but now *they* can't seem to sit still for a bite. Every mealtime seems like a battle: you chase after them with food, begging them to have some as they flit from activity to activity.

On Day 1, I said that children have no concept of healthfulness. You may have been forced to eat "what's good for you" (which usually means "vegetables"). You know only too well that being forced to eat something backfires – you still approach the foods that you were forced to eat with trepidation. You are reluctant to press this onto your own children.

Children do not eat food because it is good for them, and so it is pointless to use this argument with them. Children eat because food tastes good and because they are familiar with it. They eat a portion of food because everybody else is eating that food. And they will eat the food again if nothing bad happens to them after they have eaten it. They are even more likely to eat it again if something *good* happens to them after they have eaten it – for instance, if they feel good or they get praise[1].

You may be one of the unlucky few who experienced an eating disorder in the past and still find mealtimes difficult. For you, a healthy relationship with food seems an impossible dream[2]. If this is you, and you are blaming yourself, stop. You cannot make a child have a healthy relationship with food. All you can do is to steer them in the right direction.

Do the exercises in this book as best as you can. Do not rely on your child to heal your own relationship with food. If you are still struggling with food, then seek help. Do what you need to do to support your child into a healthy relationship with food and mealtimes.

## Day 2: Try this at home

The exercise today is less about your child's relationship with food, and more about how your own childhood food experiences have shaped your attitude to food.

- Which food habits and mealtime rules come from your own upbringing?
- Are these helpful in your own family, or might a change in these rules and habits make mealtimes less stressful?

I have filled in two examples to show you what I mean. The first is an example of a helpful habit in a family that I might want to keep. The second is a less helpful habit that I might want to change.

| Rule or habit from my own childhood | How has this affected me as an adult? |
|---|---|
| *I had to finish everything on my plate. Everybody did before we could get down from the table.* | *Now I find it hard to stop eating when full. I must finish everything on my plate, and usually on the table too!* |
| *We had a biscuit tin and we had to ask permission to have something from it. But our grown-up brother could help himself and used to tease us with it. The tin was this special thing that you had to be special to touch.* | *I turn to biscuits for comfort when I'm feeling down or stressed or tired and worn out, and any time I need pepping up.* |
| | |
| | |
| | |

| How do I apply this in my own family? | Is this still helpful? Or not? | How could I start to change this rule or habit today? |
|---|---|---|
| *I promised that I would never make my children finish everything on their plates. I stuck to this.* | *I think so. It means the children learn to listen to their appetites and stop when they are full.* | *I think this habit is helpful and doesn't need changing.* |
| *I promised to never make my own children beg for permission and they can help themselves from the biscuit tin and snack cupboard whenever they want.* | *I think they eat too many of these now. I'm sure this is part of the problem at dinner time – they have eaten biscuits and snacks and just aren't hungry for their tea.* | *Maybe I should limit the number of biscuits they eat, so they will be hungrier at teatime. I could say that they are only allowed one or two biscuits, and then put the tin away, out of sight.* |
| | | |
| | | |
| | | |

# Day 3: Children Are Good at Growing!

When a toddler refuses to eat, a parent's main concern is that they will not get enough nutrition to be well and healthy.

As with many things related to our children's nutrition, logic is often trumped by our innate survival instincts. It doesn't help to be told, when your child refuses a meal, 'Don't worry, they will be getting enough energy to grow!'

This is, however, exactly what I'm about to say.

It can be particularly alarming for parents of toddlers when a child's appetite seems to tail off after their first year. They drank milk, and then ate solids, without issue. But once they turned one, their appetite seemed to drop off.

This is perfectly normal, as the child's growth slows down compared to when they were a baby. Nevertheless, it often worries parents – particularly first-time parents who are unsure of what to expect.

Children who are healthy will eat as much as they need to grow. This is particularly the case for younger children – if they have more calorific food, then they will eat less of it[1]. Young children will also eat more on one day, and less on another, as they regulate their intake to their needs.

## How do we assess a child's growth?

Children's growth is measured on growth charts. In the UK, we use the UK-WHO growth reference charts. These charts were based on the child growth standards published by the World Health Organisation (WHO). WHO measured healthy girls and boys from six different countries as they grew.

You can download and print growth charts from the Royal College of Paediatrics and Child Health website, free of charge. Just follow this link: *www.rcpch.ac.uk/resources/growth-charts*.

In the US and Australia you use the WHO growth charts (*www.cdc.gov/growthcharts/who_charts.htm*) for infants and children aged 0 to 2 years and the CDC growth charts (*www.cdc.gov/growthcharts/clinical_charts.htm*) for children aged 2 and older.

The growth charts are pink for girls and blue for boys. In the UK, you will probably have seen these charts in your child's "red book" but may not have paid much attention to your child's growth since, as they seemed to be growing at about the same pace as their classmates.

The growth charts show a range of heights and weights at different ages. These are the lines that make up the growth charts. **Age** is on the bottom (X-axis), and the sides (Y-axes) show **height** (the top lines) and **weight** (the bottom lines).

All children are different. Some are taller and others shorter; some are a heavier build and others are slimmer. The growth charts allow for this, with some children at the bottom end of the lines for each age ($0.4^{th}$ centile) and others at the top end for each age ($99.6^{th}$ centile).

### What do the centiles mean?

If we lined up 100 children who were growing normally, with the tallest child on the left and the shortest child on the right, we would have a range of heights. The tallest of these children, furthest on the left, would be on the $99.6^{th}$ centile for our group. The shortest child, furthest away on the right, would be on the $0.4^{th}$ centile. The child who was exactly in the middle of these 100 children would be in the middle of our row, straight ahead of us, on the $50^{th}$ centile. Half of the children would be taller than the $50^{th}$ centile child, and the other half shorter than the $50^{th}$ centile child.

Basically, any of these heights and weights are perfectly normal. Health services may worry if a child is 'more than two centile lines apart'.

For example, if your child is on the $50^{th}$ centile for height and on the $99.6^{th}$ for weight (four centile lines apart), this indicates that they are probably overweight, i.e. heavier than they are tall.

If your child is on the $50^{th}$ centile for height and on the $2^{nd}$ for weight (three centile lines apart), then this indicates that they are underweight. This is likely to be investigated by a doctor, to make sure there is no medical explanation.

However, a child who is on the $2^{nd}$ centile for height and on the $0.4^{th}$ for weight (and has always been) is both short and slim, and this would not usually be of concern. This would only be a worry if this child has "dropped" in centiles from previous measurements, meaning that they were previously on a higher centile line. This, too, is likely to be investigated by a doctor, to rule out any undiagnosed medical condition.

> In most cases, children who are fussy with their food are growing perfectly normally. If your child is not growing as expected, or has "dropped" from their centile line, you must make an appointment for them to see a GP or doctor.

You might have noticed that your child's midwife put a cross or dot and circle each time your child was weighed and measured. This is called "plotting" growth. It allows us to see a child's growth trend line at a glance.

You will probably notice, if you plot your child's height and weight, that they keep following their centile line, staying on the same line they were on when they were much younger.

### Don't count on calories

Parents often worry that their child is not getting enough nutrition, so they offer alternative meals and treat foods just to get them to eat something (anything!). Usually, in fact, these children are growing perfectly well. Sometimes, they have even gone up a centile line or two in weight.

I often explain to parents that making sure a child gets enough energy as calories is not the most vital thing (although it is, of course, important too!) if they are growing well. It could be more worrying for a child to eat too many unhealthy foods as their parents try to get more nutrition, or calories, in. This often means that they will not be getting the vitamins, minerals and other essential nutrients that they need. We will revisit this on Day 9 when I talk about the importance of iron for young children.

### Changing expectations

One last note about our expectations of healthy weight in children, and how they have changed in recent years. Many parents fear that their child is underweight because they look thinner than their classmates. A child at a healthy weight may well appear too thin compared to classmates because more children are now overweight. When parents see their child's height and weight plotted, they are often surprised to find out that their child is growing perfectly normally.

## Day 3: Try this at home

Today's exercise is a practical one. I would like you to download and print the right growth chart for your child (here's that link again: *www.rcpch.ac.uk/resources/growth-charts* in the UK or *www.cdc.gov/growthcharts/who_charts.htm* in the US and Australia). Remember, blue for boys and pink for girls. Make sure you get the right age group, too: there are charts for children aged 0-4 and different charts for children aged 2-18.

1. Weigh and measure your child and plot their height and weight on the growth chart
2. Where are they? Are you surprised? (Many parents are surprised to find that their child is right where they ought to be.)
3. If you still have your child's red book, or any other height and weight records, check today's height and weight against records from the first few weeks and months. Are there any surprises here? (Some parents find that their child has gained a weight centile, which they are not usually expecting.)

# Day 4: Do Children Need to Eat Differently from Their Parents?

Centuries ago, children would usually eat a poorer version of what their parents ate. The workingmen of the household, who were bringing in the family livelihood, would get the best food, including the food with the most protein.

All this changed in Victorian times when attitudes shifted, and children became little people with their own special needs. Many diets were prescribed specifically for children. These often consisted of quite bland foods[1].

Today, the general consensus is that young children can pretty much eat the same as their parents.

There are some exceptions. For example, we don't recommend whole nuts for children younger than 5, because of the risk of choking. Foods that are around the size of a child's airway can also pose a risk if they get inhaled and stuck. Other foods that might present a choking hazard include:

- Seeds
- Popcorn/whole kernels of corn
- Dry cereal flakes
- Crisps
- Small pieces of raw carrot, celery, apple and pears
- Raw peas
- Hard sweets, jellybeans, and other hard pastilles

More tips to reduce the chance of choking

- Cut pitted cherries and olives, cherry tomatoes and grapes into halves, or quarters.
- Chop meat, poultry, sausages, and other food into small pieces.
- Avoid sticky foods like marshmallows. Spread nut butter thinly onto crackers or toast.
- Never leave children under 5 alone while they are eating in case they choke.
- If children are in a highchair, always strap them in.
- Insist that children sit down to eat and drink; they should not be lying, walking or running around.

When offered a wide variety of foods, it is often surprising the range of foods a toddler will accept, manage and enjoy. Their range of agreeable foods might include spicy foods and garlic, for example.

## Unnecessary distinctions?

Despite society's more modern approach to children's diets, some remnants of old-fashioned views still remain, which may be amplified by the time constraints and flexible working patterns of modern families.

It is not uncommon for children (or even one child), to eat separately (usually earlier) than one or both parents. I will come back to this point on Day 24, where we explore the importance of role modelling for children's eating habits.

Food manufacturers perpetuate the myth that children's food is somehow special. Cartoon and TV characters often appear in advertising, while the products are wrapped up in fun packaging designed to appeal to children (or their parents!). Foods and drinks are manipulated so that taste and texture will appeal to younger palettes (as we discussed on Day 1).

Young children have far fewer reference points than adults when making food choices. As adults, we might consider the healthfulness of a food or drink when making a choice. We might also consider price, how simple it is to prepare, and maybe even ease of storage. Children, however, have only three reference points when it comes to their food choices:

1) Taste and texture (likeability)
2) Their observation of their role models engaging with this food (have I seen Mum/Dad/ siblings/peers eat this and what was their reaction when they did?)
3) The consequences they experience when they try a food (do I get attention, and what kind of attention? Does it make me sick?)

**Why does it matter?**

Foods aimed at children are often more expensive than the adult versions and frequently contain more sugar.

We are often lured into buying foods aimed at children because experience tells us they are more likely to eat it than an adult or homemade equivalent – and we don't have the time or energy for another mealtime battle.

With the exception of some of the hazardous foods mentioned above, young children do not need to eat very differently from their parents.

They are still developing the skills needed to chew and swallow effectively and so will need some foods (e.g. meat) to be moist and/or chopped to help with chewing, especially until they have all of their teeth. As young children prefer:

- Food that they have eaten before
- Food that others are eating
- And, of course, food that they like

it has to be tasty.

## Day 4: Try this at home

Select three foods that you have at home that you bought especially because you thought there was a greater chance that your child would eat it.

Look at the label for the amount of sugar in the food per 100g (or 100ml if it is a liquid). Find the price for each of the three foods (supermarket websites are great for this).

Now, see if you can find an adult equivalent for each. Compare the price and sugar content between the "child" and "adult" versions of the foods.

You might find the chart below helpful to order your thoughts, or you may prefer to do it in your head. I have completed two examples to show you what I mean. As you can see, there is a significant difference in both price and sugar content.

| 1. What made you buy the product aimed at children?<br>2. Is there an equivalent adult version?<br>3. How does this compare for grams of sugar per 100g?<br>4. How does it compare price-wise? | | | | | | |
|---|---|---|---|---|---|---|
| Child food | Price* | Grams of sugar per 100g | Why did I buy this? | Adult equivalent | Price | Grams sugar per 100g |
| Petit Filous Magic Squares yoghurts | 31p per 100g | 10.8g† | Designed for kids | Own brand smooth fruit yoghurt | 17.1p per 100g | 10.0g |
| Fruit Bowl Branded Strawberry Peelers | £2.81 per 100g | 58g | The packet says they are made with real fruit and count as 1 of your 5 a day | Own brand dried apricots | £1.25 per 100g | 36.5g |
| | | | | | | |
| | | | | | | |

* Prices correct on 15th June 2019.

*† I note fructose is being used in many food products across many brands recently. Fructose is sweeter than sucrose (table sugar) and so less can be used to achieve the same sweet taste. This means that the grams of sugar per 100g of the product will be less, which will appeal to many consumers looking to eat less sugar, as we will be checking labels for g sugar/100g. Sucrose is made up of one molecule of fructose and one molecule of glucose. It has been argued that fructose is the most harmful part of table sugar (see, for example, Robert Lustig, 2013. "Fat Chance: Beating the Odds against Sugar, Processed Food, Obesity, and Disease." and my own book "Sugar Counter for Health: The Smart Person's Guide to Hidden Sugars", 2016.). So, while replacing some sucrose with fructose may mean that the grams of sugar per 100g appears less on the food label, it might not mean that a particular food is healthier.*

# Day 5: What Children Need to Eat

Dietitians usually talk about food in groups of foods. In the UK, we use the Eatwell Guide (below). You may have seen copies up in doctor's surgeries, children's centres and family clinics.

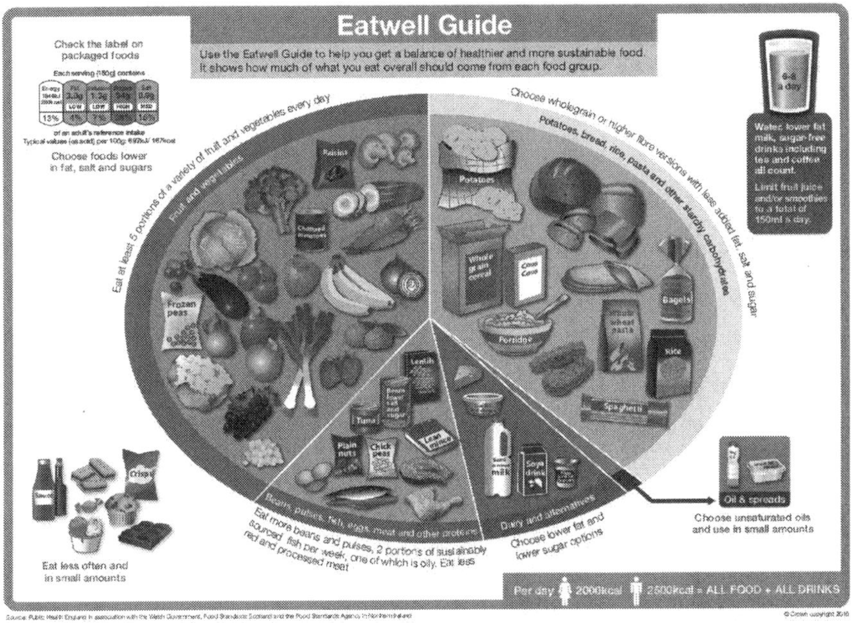


The US also uses a plate model, called MyPlate. Australians may be familiar with another plate model: the Australian Dietary Guidelines.

In many European countries, the food groups are represented as a pyramid.

## Why do we use food groups?

Whether plate, pyramid or something else entirely, we use these models to group foods that provide similar nutrients together.

## What does this have to do with getting your child to eat more?

Using food groups can help you get an idea of whether your toddler is refusing food to an extent that might cause a *nutritional* problem; or refusing to an extent that is more a problem of variety and social acceptance.

If your child is eating enough food from each food group to get the nutrition that she needs, it can take a whole load of pressure off you as a parent. This reduced stress will make applying the principles of the rest of the book a lot easier.

## Wiggle room

The beauty of food groups is that you don't necessarily have to eat *everything* in one food group to have a good diet.

It doesn't actually matter, from a nutritional point of view, if I never eat brussels sprouts again. As long as I am eating plenty of vegetables, including some brassica and green leafy veg, it will make no difference to my nutritional state if a brussels sprout never passes my lips again for the rest of my life.

Similarly, if your child just refuses to eat hummus, but will eat other foods with calcium, iron and even baked beans and kidney beans in chilli, then it doesn't really matter *from a nutritional point of view* that she simply refuses to try just a tiny bit of hummus. It may still be a problem from a *social* point of view if the rest of the family loves hummus and eats it by the bucketful. Nevertheless, it is not a nutritional concern.

I am hoping that by understanding the food groups it might make you less anxious as a parent if your child is missing a few foods. If you are less anxious that she is missing out, then it will be easier to apply the principles in the rest of this book.

## Day 5: Try this at home

### Foods and servings

In the table below, I have outlined how many servings from each of the food groups children aged 1-4 need. I have taken this information from the First Steps Nutrition Trust and from the British Nutrition Foundation's 5-5-3-2 guide to portion sizes for toddlers.

First Steps Nutrition Trust is a UK public health nutrition charity. It has some excellent, practical resources for meal planning for families with toddlers. I particularly like their *Eating well recipe book: Simple, cost-effective ideas for the whole family*. This booklet has a range of family recipes that can be adapted to any age. Each recipe is adapted to different age groups (including serving sizes) and photographed. You can visit their website here: *www.firststepsnutrition.org*.

The British Nutrition Foundation's 5-5-3-2 guide to portion sizes for toddlers recommends 5 servings of fruit or veg each day, 5 servings of starchy foods, 3 of dairy foods and 2 of protein foods (3 servings of protein foods if your child is vegetarian). You can find the guide here: *bit.ly/FussyDay5*.

| Note: 1 dessertspoon = 2/3rd American tablespoon | | | |
|---|---|---|---|
| Food group and servings per day | Which foods are included | Example foods and toddler portion sizes | Notes |
| **Starchy foods**<br><br>5 servings per day | All types of **bread**, including chapattis, naan bread, roti, rolls, bagels, pitta bread, wraps, and tortilla<br><br>**Potatoes or sweet potatoes**<br><br>**Yam, plantain, cocoyam, cassava,** and other starchy root vegetables<br><br>**Pasta and noodles**<br><br>**Rice**<br><br>**Other grains** such as pearl barley, couscous or bulgur wheat, maize (polenta), quinoa and cornmeal<br><br>**Breakfast cereals** – low-sugar, low-salt cereals such as porridge, puffed wheat, wheat biscuits, crisped rice or flaked wheat. | ½-1 slice of bread<br><br>1-2 rice cakes or oatcakes<br><br>3-5 dessertspoons no-added-sugar breakfast cereal<br><br>1-3 dessertspoons mashed potato<br><br>2-4 dessertspoons cooked pasta or rice<br><br>2-4 potato wedges | Look for lower-salt bread.<br><br>*<br><br>Avoid processed potato products like waffles or smiley faces.<br><br>*<br><br>Avoid dried or canned ready prepared pasta in sauce, as these are very salty.<br><br>*<br><br>Avoid fried rice or flavoured dried rice in packets.<br><br>*<br><br>Avoid sugary breakfast cereals. Look for those that have no added sugar. |

| | | | |
|---|---|---|---|
| **Fruit & vegetables**<br><br>5 servings per day | All types of **fresh, frozen and canned vegetables**<br><br>All types of **salad vegetables**<br><br>All types of **fresh fruit**<br><br>All types of **canned fruit** in juice<br><br>**Stewed fruit**<br><br>**Dried fruit** | ½-2 dessertspoons raisins<br><br>¼-1 banana<br><br>3-8 grapes<br><br>½-2 dessertspoons peas<br><br>½-2 dessertspoons broccoli<br><br>¼-½ medium apple<br><br>1-3 cherry tomatoes<br><br>2-6 vegetable sticks<br><br>2-4 dessertspoons canned fruit | Avoid vegetables canned with added salt and sugar.<br><br>*<br><br>Avoid fruit canned in syrup.<br><br>*<br><br>If the fruit to be stewed is sour, add a little apple juice, or mix with sweeter fruit.<br><br>*<br><br>Avoid dried fruit with added sugar and vegetable oil.<br><br>*<br><br>Serve dried fruit with meals and not as snacks. This is to reduce the risk of dental decay from sticky dried fruit. |

| | | | |
|---|---|---|---|
| **Dairy foods**<br><br>3 servings per day | **Breastmilk**<br><br>**Milk**<br><br>Whole (full fat) cows' milk (or other whole animal milk) can be used as the main milk drink from the age of 12 months.<br><br>Over-2s can have semi-skimmed milk if they are good eaters.<br><br>**Non-dairy milk alternatives**<br><br>For children who avoid dairy products, unsweetened calcium-fortified soya milk alternative can be given as the main milk drink from 1 year of age. Other unsweetened fortified milk drinks such as almond, oat, hemp or coconut milk can be used.<br><br>**Cheese**<br><br>Cheese is high in salt, so use in small amounts.<br><br>**Yoghurt and fromage frais**<br><br>Choose plain, full-fat, unsweetened versions. Soya-milk-based or coconut-milk-based alternatives are available for those on dairy-free diets. | 1 beaker of milk (100ml)<br><br>1 pot of yoghurt (125ml)<br><br>1 cheese triangle<br><br>2-4 dessertspoons rice pudding<br><br>1-3 dessertspoons cheese sauce<br><br>2 small yoghurt tubes | Avoid unpasteurised milk.<br><br>*<br><br>Avoid milk drinks with flavours and added sugar.<br><br>*<br><br>Avoid "growing up" milk or toddler milk.<br><br>*<br><br>**Do not serve rice milk to children under 5 years.**<br><br>*<br><br>All milk alternatives (including soya milk) are much lower in energy, and can be lower in some important nutrients, than full-fat animal milk. Care needs to be taken that the rest of the diet provides adequate energy.<br><br>*<br><br>Avoid unpasteurised cheese and mould-ripened (blue-vein) cheeses.<br><br>*<br><br>Avoid yoghurts and fromage frais that have a high sugar content. If the yoghurt or fromage frais has more than 15g of sugar per 100g, it is a high-sugar option. Instead, add fresh fruit to natural yoghurt or fromage frais. |

| | | | |
|---|---|---|---|
| **Protein foods**<br><br>2 servings per day (3 if your child is vegetarian) | **Meat and poultry**<br><br>**Fish**<br><br>**Eggs**<br><br>All sorts of **pulses,** including butter beans, kidney beans, chickpeas, lentils or baked beans<br><br>**Ground nuts** – such as smooth peanut butter, cashew or almond butter<br><br>**Crushed seeds** or ground seeds – such as sunflower seeds, pumpkin seeds or tahini<br><br>**Meat alternatives** –<br><br>such as soya mince/ textured vegetable protein, Quorn or tofu | 2-3 dessertspoons chickpeas, kidney beans, dhal, lentils or beans<br><br>2-4 dessertspoons cooked minced meat<br><br>1-2 fish fingers<br><br>2-3 dessertspoons baked beans<br><br>½-1 poached, boiled or fried egg<br><br>Peanut butter on bread or toast | Avoid processed meat and fish products that are high in fat and salt, such as crumb-coated products, burgers, pies, sausages, and canned meats.<br><br>*<br><br>Make sure fish dishes are free of bones.<br><br>*<br><br>Eggs stamped with the British Lion mark can be eaten raw or lightly cooked. All other eggs (including eggs not from a hen) should be cooked until the white and yolk are firm.<br><br>*<br><br>Look for canned pulses with no added salt and sugar.<br><br>*<br><br>Choose lower-salt and low-sugar baked beans.<br><br>*<br><br>Avoid processed meat alternatives (such as vegetarian sausages, burgers and pies), as these can be high in salt. |

**Exercise**

For each meal or snack, offer a small amount of a type of food (or foods) you know your child likes, and then one or two new foods. On Day 6, we will talk more about mealtime routines.

For three whole days, count/tally/record each time your child has a portion from one of the food groups. I have provided an example to demonstrate.

At the end of the three days, count up how many servings of each food group your child has each day. How does this compare to the recommended amount?

*Example record:*

| | Day 1 | Day 2 | Day 3 | Total |
|---|---|---|---|---|
| Starchy foods<br>Daily target: 5 | \|\|\|\| | \|\|\|\| | \|\|\|\| | Recommended total: 15<br>12 |
| Fruit and vegetables<br>Daily target: 5 | ~~1~~ ~~2~~ 3 4 5 | ~~1~~ ~~2~~ ~~3~~ ~~4~~ ~~5~~ | ~~1~~ ~~2~~ ~~3~~ ~~4~~ 5 | Recommended total: 15<br>10 |
| Milk and dairy foods<br>Daily target: 3 | 1 2 (3) | 1 2 (3) | (1) 2 3 | Recommended total: 9<br>7 |
| Protein foods<br>Daily target: 2 (3 if vegetarian) | 1 | 3 | 2 | Recommended total: 6 (9 if vegetarian)<br>6 |

*Your child's record:*

| | Day 1 | Day 2 | Day 3 | Total |
|---|---|---|---|---|
| Starchy foods<br><br>Daily target: 5 | | | | Recommended total: 15 |
| | | | | |
| Fruit and vegetables<br><br>Daily target: 5 | | | | Recommended total: 15 |
| | | | | |
| Milk and dairy foods<br><br>Daily target: 3 | | | | Recommended total: 9 |
| | | | | |
| Protein foods<br><br>Daily target: 2 (3 if vegetarian) | | | | Recommended total: 6 (9 if vegetarian) |
| | | | | |

# Day 6: Mealtime Routines

Children need regular, planned meals and snacks[1].

Younger children rely on parents to provide regular meals and snacks. They need to be *able* to rely on this – to know that food is going to be available at regular intervals. This means your child should be offered three regular meals and two or three planned snacks each day at fairly consistent times.

I recommend three meals and two to three snacks for several reasons.

- So that young children have several opportunities to meet their calorie needs.
- It helps take away the anxiety for parents if their child eats very little at a particular mealtime – it's not too long until another one is on its way. Mealtimes should be relaxed and enjoyable affairs, not a battleground.
- The other reason is that, contrary to popular belief, being famished doesn't help young children to eat better (more on this below).

## Smoothing the way

It can help if you set the tone and expectations for the meal that is due. Alert your child that it is time to eat soon and then, when it is, establish a mealtime routine that is predictable and calming.

Wash hands (all of you!), enlist your child to help (as far as he is able) to set the table, sit down and get ready to eat.

Don't get emotional. Young children are clued in to the atmosphere at mealtimes and high emotion sends a negative message about mealtimes. This may require an Oscar-winning performance on your behalf, but the effort is worth the outcome: relaxed and enjoyable family meals.

Although it is never a good idea to allow children to beg for food in between meals, you do need to provide regular, planned snacks. While grazing will spoil a child's appetite, a planned snack between meals does not.

When children, especially younger children, are very hungry, they eat less, not more. It is always best if they start each meal or snack *hungry*, but not *starving*. Being starving stops you from concentrating so well on things – remember, young children have to concentrate on the skill of eating. (For this reason, I also recommend that children are not exhausted before a mealtime or snack either.)

Having a regular routine of meals and planned snacks will also help you put the rest of the techniques in this book into action. You will be less anxious if your child refuses to eat, or eats very little, as there are never long gaps without food being offered.

## What is a snack?

Some parents I have worked with have been dubious about the advice to include regular, planned snacks. They have said that snacks are unhealthy and that these will lead to their child becoming overweight.

A planned snack is not the same as grazing. Planned snacks prevent *unplanned* snacks, which are usually less healthy. Planned snacks also prevent begging for food and grazing between meals.

We have come to associate the word "snack" with heavily processed, pre-packaged snack-sized foods. These are often of low quality and low nutritional value.

When *I* talk about a "snack", I mean a mini-meal – a small amount of normal food. This mini-meal will probably have fewer components and variety than a standard meal.

For example, there may be only two or three foods in a snack, rather than the four, five or six you might expect to serve as a main meal. Some examples:

- A piece of toast with peanut butter and a small glass of milk
- Chopped fruit and a few small pieces of cheese or ham
- Chopped carrot and a breadstick served with hummus for dipping

There are lots and lots of options out there. It doesn't have to be a sugary fromage frais, a packet of cheesy crisp snacks or a cereal bar (although these can, of course, be served from time to time).

As well as being healthier, offering small servings of normal food for a snack will also be less expensive than commercial snack foods.

Finally, having a snack is not the same as grazing. Constantly eating (grazing) and/or eating (often mindlessly) while walking about the house or doing other things and being given food on demand teaches young children to eat out of boredom.

## Avoid distractions

Generally, children eat poorly when they are distracted by TV, games etc.

Although a popular theory is that adults eat more when we are distracted (so-called "mindless eating"), children tend to eat less well. This is because they are still learning the skills of eating and need to concentrate on what they are doing.

There are some exceptions to this. Some children with sensory processing issues may eat better with distractions, but this will not help most children. I remember one mum who told me that she could only get her 5-year-old son to eat if she put the iPad on. She did not eat with him; instead, putting his food out while she got on with other jobs. This young boy was otherwise developing normally with no identified sensory issues - the team suspected that he just didn't like eating on his own.

My message is that most children fare best if they focus on eating at meals and snacks in the company of role models. In this way, they learn to savour and enjoy food, how to behave at the table and how to listen to their appetite cues telling them when they have had enough.

## Limit mealtimes to 20-30 minutes.

I do not recommend that a child is made to sit at the table until his food is finished. This is counterproductive. It draws mealtimes out, makes them emotionally charged events, upsets future meals and often leads to tears and tantrums.

Young children have short attention spans while adults sometimes like to sit at the table beyond the meal to relax or talk. Making a child stay at the table is just too much to ask. Limit mealtimes or snacks to 20-30 minutes maximum. A snack may only need to be ten minutes.

This doesn't mean that *everybody* has to get up from the table – feel free to chat with your partner! Just don't make your child stay at the table for longer than this. Half-an-hour, done, down from the table and on to whatever is the next activity on his agenda.

## Day 6: Try this at home

Compile a list of 10 - 12 healthy snacks for your child. It might help to think of about three or four that can be packed up for when you are both out and about. I have filled in one line as an example.

| Snack ideas |
|---|
| e.g. *Oatcake spread thinly with peanut butter and some pieces of chopped fruit.* |
| 1. |
| 2. |
| 3. |
| 4. |
| 5. |
| 6. |
| 7. |
| 8. |
| 9. |
| 10. |
| 11. |
| 12. |

On Day 5, when we looked at what young children should eat, I mentioned the First Steps Nutrition Trust. They also have an excellent snack resource, with loads of ideas for healthy snacks. Most of the snack ideas include starchy food, fruit or vegetables and a protein or dairy food, so they cover all the food groups. You can find it here (in PDF format): *bit.ly/FussyDay6*.

# Day 7: Milk, Juice and Yoghurt

Many children who are referred to me for fussy eating advice are drinking way too much milk or juice and eating far too much yoghurt.

Drinking, especially from a bottle, is easier than chewing and eating. That means that many children will just drink milk and juice or eat yoghurts if they get the chance, meeting their energy needs with liquids.

Researchers from the *Gateshead Millennium Baby Study* in the UK analysed 455 questionnaires completed by parents of 30-month-old children. The results showed that 13% of the children studied preferred drinks to food[1]. The authors concluded that excessive milk drinking may be a cause of low appetite at mealtimes.

## Why does it matter?

Children can fill up on milk, which leaves less room for food – especially iron-rich foods.

Researchers studying a subset of children in the *Avon Longitudinal Study of Parents and Children* (also known as the Children of the 90s study), showed that the children who were fussy eaters drank more milk than their non-fussy counterparts. This was particularly obvious for those children who were fussy at 3 ½ years old, and still fussy aged 7 ½ years[2].

Sipping milk (or juice) from a bottle throughout the day does not allow a young child to become hungry and build up an appetite for iron-rich solid food[3]. Children who are given excessive amounts of milk (and juice) to drink are more likely to be iron-deficient[4].

I would include sweetened yoghurts in this classification. Yoghurt is easy to eat – some children I have met ate several yoghurts, usually sweetened, every day. Broadly speaking, foods that contain calcium will not be iron-rich. Excessive amounts of calcium also interfere with how iron is absorbed. By taking in too much dairy, your child will be consuming and absorbing less iron.

The First Steps Nutrition Trust (my go-to resource for toddler and child feeding guidelines!), recommends that:

- At 1-2 years old, children should be offered about 400ml (14oz) of cows' milk per day.
- Children aged 2-4 probably need about 300-350ml (10½ - 12oz) of milk per day (they will be eating bigger portions at meals, so will need less milk).

As explained on Day 5, children over 1 only need three servings of dairy foods each day to meet their calcium needs. Any more than this and your toddler may fill up on milk instead of getting more practice with solid food.

## Drinking from a bottle

Many young children who are referred to me for fussy eating advice are still drinking from a bottle. Most have moved on to cups or beakers for water (and for juice and squash if they drink this). But even those who are able to drink from a cup or beaker are still drinking their milk from a bottle.

This makes it harder to offer only the right amount of milk. Bottle drinking and sucking can be very comforting – and it is often the *comfort* that a child is seeking, rather than satisfying her thirst or hunger.

Drinking from a bottle can also have a negative effect on how a child learns to eat and to drink from a cup.

### Oro-motor skills

The coordination of the actions needed to chew food, move it through the mouth and swallow it are called 'oro-motor' skills. Bottle drinking uses an entirely different set of muscles and oro-motor reflexes than cup drinking.

The muscles and oro-motor reflexes that are used for cup drinking are helpful for eating. Those used for bottle drinking are not.

As adults, we take eating and drinking for granted. After all, once we have reached 30 years old, we have had…

(30 years x 5 meals or snacks per day x 365 days per year)

… nearly 50,000 opportunities to practice eating and drinking. No wonder we are so good at it!

Young children still have to learn this important skill. Think about some of the actions we no longer have to consider:

- Flattening your tongue to allow you to put a spoon in your mouth (a very different movement to pushing your tongue to the roof of your mouth to press on the teat of a bottle)
- Moving solid food around in your mouth as you chew – and get the food into just the right size, shape and texture to swallow (swallowing a mouthful of liquid that is delivered straight to the back of your mouth is a different skill entirely).

Drinking from a cup or beaker helps a child to develop some of the movements needed to eat solid food, like closing her lips and keeping them sealed to stop spilling.

## When to ditch the bottle

In the UK, public health recommendations suggest that, by the time babies are 12 months, they should no longer be drinking from a bottle with a teat. Any longer than this and your child is at risk of tooth decay and other dental problems, as well as problems with speech[5].

If you're bottle-feeding, it's a good idea to start introducing a cup from about six months old. By the time your baby is 1, they should have stopped using bottles with teats. Otherwise, they may find it hard to break the habit of comfort sucking on a bottle.

A beaker with a free-flow lid (without a non-spill valve) is better than a bottle or beaker with a teat. Drinks flow very slowly through a teat, which means that the child spends a lot of time with the teat in her mouth. Using an open cup or a free-flow cup helps your baby learn to sip rather than suck, which is better for her teeth.

### Gently does it

If your child seems particularly attached to her bottle, you could:

- Let her pick out a special drinking cup when you go shopping.
- Create a story to convince her why the bottle isn't a good idea (an inspirational one; not a scary one!).
- Clear out all the bottles in your house. It can be confusing for a child if they are told they cannot have a bottle until you are really tired and your willpower crumbles.
- Give her lots of praise for drinking from a cup.
- If you keep getting asked for a bottle, find out what your child really needs or wants and offer that instead. If your child is thirsty, offer a drink in a cup. If she is hungry, is it time for a snack? If it is comfort, offer hugs. If your child is bored, sit down and play instead.

If you choose a sippy cup, don't let your child use it past the age of 18-24 months. Using a sippy cup past this age can cause delayed muscle development involving the tongue. It also interferes with the correct eruption of teeth. The correct eruption of teeth is important for your child's bite, correct positioning of the tongue and, eventually, speech.

### Night-time bottle feeding and milk drinking

Night-time bottle feeding and milk drinking can be a particularly hard habit to break.

Many young children learn to associate the bottle or milk with bedtime. They may find it hard to go to sleep without.

If you use a bottle or breastfeed to get your child to sleep at bedtime, it teaches your toddler that they need the milk to fall asleep. When you offer a bottle of milk during the night, it reinforces the idea that they can only get *back* to sleep with milk. Rather than become less likely to wake, your toddler may instead begin to wake, wanting a bottle more frequently. I have met toddlers who were getting so many calories from night-time milk that they didn't eat well during the day.

Parents choose different ways of doing away with night-time bottles and milk drinks. Some choose to go cold turkey, perhaps creating a gentle story about why the bottle must go.

Other parents prefer a more gradual approach. They dilute the milk a little more each night until the bottle is all water. Some young children lose interest at this point (although this isn't always the case).

If you chose to dilute your child's milk, you could dilute the milk in the bottle with water 50/50 for the first few days, gradually increasing the amount until the entire bottle is water.

Or you could go for a more scientific approach, by using the following plan:

| | |
|---|---|
| Night 1 | 25% water and 75% milk |
| Night 2 | 50% water and 50% milk |
| Night 3 | 75% water and 25% milk |
| Night 4 | 100% water |

Yet another way is to reduce the amount of milk in the bottles offered or reduce the time of breastfeeding over a few nights.

Here are a few other tips to help break the night-time bottle habit:

- Have the milk sitting up rather than lying down, before getting into bed. Your child could have this drink sitting on your knee while you read a story.
- When her drink is finished, clean teeth and maybe have another story in bed.
- Allow 5-10 minutes of awake time after the milk is finished, so your toddler isn't relying on the milk itself to become drowsy and fall asleep.
- Don't let your child fall asleep while breastfeeding or having a bottle if you want them to learn to sleep without a milk drink.

## Skimmed milk or full-fat milk?

Should you give your child skimmed, semi-skimmed or full-fat milk?

In the UK, we recommend that children *can* be offered semi-skimmed milk from the age of two. Skimmed milk *can* be offered to children from the age of five.

Guidelines in the US are more low-fat friendly and recommend that children *should* be switched to reduced-fat milk once they are two years old. It is recommended that overweight toddlers are switched to low-fat milk even earlier, after their first birthday.

In Australia, the Australian Healthy Food Guide says that reduced-fat or low-fat milk is suitable for toddlers over 2 years old.

Guidelines aside, I tend to come down on the same side as Ellyn Satter on this point. Satter is a fellow dietitian, a counsellor and the author of several books on child and infant feeding and weaning. She suggests that children should drink full-fat milk[6], arguing that they need fat to meet their high-energy needs.

I agree. In fact, in 2016, a research group in Toronto, Canada published the results of their research into the milk-drinking habits of 2,745 children between 2 and 6 years old. They found that drinking lower-fat milk was associated with higher BMI scores[7]. Of course, we can't be sure whether drinking lower-fat milk makes a child more likely to be overweight, or whether a child has been put on to lower-fat milk because she is overweight. Maybe there is a family disposition to being heavier.

In any event, fat makes us feel full and satisfied and keeps food in our stomachs for longer. The authors of the study believe that children who drink lower-fat milk products feel less full and so are more prone to grazing.

## Day 7: Try this at home

How many servings of milk, juice, yoghurt and commercial snack foods does your child have each day? Place a tick in the box for each serving.

| | Milk | Juice | Yoghurt | Crisps, biscuits, chocolate, sweets |
|---|---|---|---|---|
| Monday | | | | |
| Tuesday | | | | |
| Wednesday | | | | |
| Thursday | | | | |
| Friday | | | | |
| Saturday | | | | |
| Sunday | | | | |
| **Total** | | | | |

Were you surprised by the results? How does your milk and yoghurt result compare to the advice in this book on recommended amounts?

# Day 8: Vitamins & Minerals

- Research has shown that picky eaters eat fewer whole-grain foods, fewer vegetables, less fish and seafood and less meat than non-picky eaters[1].
- Picky eaters have also been shown to have a lower intake of vitamins and minerals[2].

Those facts won't come as a surprise to parents of a picky eater – but they can lead to nutritional problems.

## What could my child be missing?

Not eating whole grain foods and vegetables may lead to poor fibre intake. This can cause or contribute to constipation, which in turn can put a child off her food.

Iron-fortified grain products; green, leafy vegetables; oily fish; meat – all are excellent sources of iron, and all are on the "no-go" list for many picky eaters. Young children can be prone to iron-deficiency anaemia, which I will talk more about in the next chapter. Anaemia can make a child feel tired and listless and can also affect appetite.

Fish and seafood are important sources of many nutrients, including iodine and the omega 3 fatty acids. Both iron, iodine and omega 3 fatty acids are important for the development of the brain and neurological functioning.

Iron and zinc intakes are likely to be low if your child is a picky eater[3]. Both iron and zinc are important for appetite[4]. Poor intake of iron and zinc have both been associated with behavioural problems in young children[5], which can have a long-lasting effect as a child grows up[6].

## What about supplements?

You may be asking right now whether you should give your child a supplement or not.

Some researchers have suggested that a vitamin and mineral supplement may be a good idea for children who are fussy eaters[7]. I agree with this view, generally speaking, but *only* if you are also applying the behavioural strategies in this book to increase the number and types of food your child enjoys.

Supplements are not a quick fix – and supplements alone are not a substitute for a broad and varied diet. This is partly due to the fact that we simply don't know everything about nutrition yet. Food contains far more than the vitamins and minerals we already know about. You only have to read the news to see how often yet another compound has been discovered in food – one that can protect against cancer, or heart disease, or dementia; or one that is good for our eyes[8], for example.

Your child will still be missing out if his diet is limited.

If you suspect your child might be anaemic, it is a good idea to ask your child's doctor to check this.

## Which supplements should I consider?

The UK Department for Health recommends that all children aged over 1 year (or over 6 months if drinking less than 500ml – around a pint – of formula milk per day) should be given a supplement containing vitamins A, D and C.

If your child is a fussy eater and you decide to use a more comprehensive multivitamin and mineral product for a short while, make sure you get one that contains vitamins *and* minerals. Very often, I meet parents who have bought a vitamin product that contains no iron or other minerals.

It is always better to get a supplement that contains a range of minerals, including iron, zinc, selenium and magnesium. This is because taking a supplement of one mineral can reduce the absorption of another – for example, as we learned on Day 7, too much calcium reduces the absorption of iron.

Get an over-the-counter supplement that is right for the child's age (they usually say the age range on the box or packet). And always buy a product from a reputable source and use it as instructed.

## Zinc

Zinc is an important nutrient for children because of the links between poor zinc intake and appetite. The results of the *National Diet and Nutrition Survey in the UK*[9] show that 13% of girls and 4% of boys aged between 4 and 10 do not meet the Lower Reference Nutrient Intake (LRNI) for zinc.

The Lower Reference Nutrient Intake refers to an amount of a nutrient that is enough for those – just 2.5% of a group – who have low requirements. It can, therefore, be considered the bare minimum required, and the majority of children will need more.

This means that many more children are just not getting enough zinc in their diets.

Doctors will not routinely test zinc levels so, if you are concerned that your child is not consuming a range of foods that contain plenty of zinc and other minerals, you might want to use a multivitamin and mineral supplement until your child's diet is back on track. Good sources of zinc are listed at the end of this chapter.

If you do use a supplement, and your child is already being prescribed iron by his GP, please let your child's doctor know that you are giving him a multivitamin and mineral supplement as well.

Generally, over-the-counter vitamins and mineral products only contain small amounts of iron, but it's important to double-check with your child's doctor to make sure he isn't taking too much. It is often helpful to take the supplement bottle or packet along to an appointment, as the iron content will be listed on the back.

**Vitamin D**

Although there are small amounts of vitamin D in some foods (such as liver, egg yolks and fortified foods like spreads), we get most of our vitamin D from the action of sunlight on our skin. Getting enough vitamin D has always been a problem in the Northern hemisphere and its prevalence is rising. This is because we go outdoors less and use sunscreen more, both of which hinder the sunlight in doing its thing to make vitamin D.

Some of us may be old enough to remember being given cod liver oil as a child. This was mainly to prevent rickets – a bone disease caused by vitamin D deficiency. Inadequate amounts of vitamin D in children means the bones don't harden properly and so the legs tend to bow outwards as they grow up and bear their body weight on their legs.

The UK's National Health Service (NHS) advises that all children aged between 1 and 5 years should be given a daily supplement of vitamin D. As mentioned above, the Department of Health recommends that all children between the ages of 1 and 4 years are given a supplement containing vitamins A, C and D. (For those who are able to access Healthy Start vitamins from their Health Visitor, these contain vitamins A, C and D.)

After the age of 5, when they no longer need a supplement containing vitamins A, C and D, children (and adults!) should take a supplement of vitamin D only during the winter months. Those 'at risk' should take one all year round.

The recommended amount for children over 1 year of age, and for adults, is 10microgrammes per day.

You can get vitamin D supplements inexpensively over-the-counter from supermarkets, pharmacies and health food shops. Choose supplements that contain the vitamin in the D3 form rather than in the D2 form, as this is more effective.

*Who is 'at risk'?*

People at risk include adults and children who do not go outdoors very much and those with dark skin*. If your child falls into either of these groups, then he should be given vitamin D all year round.

## Making the supplement appealing

It can be hit-and-miss getting a fussy eater to take a vitamin and mineral supplement.

Reward charts can sometimes help. I worked for a while with a parenting behavioural specialist and have adopted her advice on reward charts: keep them brief and tangible.

Long, drawn-out charts with a reward several weeks in the future do not work for young children. They need to see rewards quickly. Perhaps a small reward for every three days that he takes his supplement?

The reward doesn't have to be large, nor expensive (and definitely not food!). Spending special time together – watching a favourite film, reading a favourite story together or going on a trip to the park – is often enough.

---

* Skin colour is relevant because vitamin D is made below the skin's layer of melanin. Melanin is what gives skin its dark colour – the more melanin you make, the darker your skin. Sunlight cannot penetrate melanin, and so those with darker skin make less vitamin D than those with fairer skin.

## Day 8: Try this at home

I have listed some of the best sources of zinc and vitamin A in children's diets below. For each day of the week, tick off each time your child has a serving of food from each of these two nutrients.

I have included vitamin A because we know that young children often do not get adequate amounts through their diets.

---

Targets: Zinc & Vitamin A

Assuming your child has the recommended three servings of dairy foods each day, he will need two or three daily servings of the other protein foods listed to get enough zinc in his diet.

In addition to full-fat milk and dairy foods, which are higher in vitamin A than lower-fat products, he will also need at least one other source of vitamin A each day. If this is impossible to achieve at the moment, then he is going to need to take vitamin A as a supplement.

Do remember that this is an average over a week – we store both zinc and vitamin A, and so we do not need to hit a daily target.

Because it can be hard to get enough vitamin A, the Department of Health in the UK recommends that all children aged 6 months to 5 years are given vitamin drops containing vitamins A, C and D. If you do this, then your child will not need a separate vitamin D supplement. And if you are giving your child a multivitamin/mineral, he will not need the vitamin drops as well.

---

We will repeat this exercise for iron in the next chapter so, if you prefer, you can do all three nutrients at the same time.

| | Zinc | | |
|---|---|---|---|
| | Monday | Tuesday | Wednesday |
| **Shellfish** e.g. oysters, crab and lobster | | | |
| **Red meat** e.g. beef and pork | | | |
| **Baked beans, chickpeas, kidney beans and green peas** | | | |
| **Yoghurt, cheese and milk** | | | |
| **Nuts and seeds** *These should be served ground or as butter for children under 5, due to the risk of choking* | | | |
| **Total** | | | |

| Zinc | | | |
|---|---|---|---|
| Thursday | Friday | Saturday | Sunday |
| | | | |
| | | | |
| | | | |
| | | | |
| | | | |
| | | | |

| | Vitamin A | | |
|---|---|---|---|
| | Monday | Tuesday | Wednesday |
| **Liver** | | | |
| **Dairy foods** e.g. butter and buttery spreads, cheese, and milk | | | |
| **Orange coloured vegetables & fruit** e.g. carrots, squash, sweet potato, apricots (especially dried), cantaloupe melon, pumpkin, and mango | | | |
| **Green leafy vegetables** e.g. kale, chard, and spinach | | | |
| **Total** | | | |

| Vitamin A | | | |
|---|---|---|---|
| Thursday | Friday | Saturday | Sunday |
| | | | |
| | | | |
| | | | |
| | | | |
| | | | |

# Day 9: Iron & Iron Deficiency Anaemia

Anaemia and sub-clinical iron deficiency affect children's learning and normal neurological development[1], their mood, their appetite and their behaviour.

It probably has a lasting effect on your child's learning and the development of her brain and nervous system[2].

Anaemic young children (often referred to me for refusing food) will usually show these signs:

- 'White as a ghost' (or, if they have dark skin, sallow and yellowy or grey and ashen) with dark circles under their eyes
- Always tired
- Irritable
- Prone to infections

## What is anaemia?

Anaemia and sub-clinical iron deficiency are a cause *and* effect of food refusal in young children.

Iron status is measured by haemoglobin and ferritin in the blood.

- Low haemoglobin indicates anaemia
- Low ferritin suggests that iron stores are low but have not yet resulted in low haemoglobin[3] (and therefore anaemia). I refer to this as sub-clinical iron deficiency.

Iron deficiency without anaemia can itself lead to problems with learning and brain development. It used to be thought this might be because iron deficiency makes children more susceptible to high blood levels of lead[4]. We now think that iron deficiency causes changes in neurotransmitters and how children's nerve cells grow and develop[5].

A haemoglobin measurement below 110g/L for children aged 1 ½ to 4 years is diagnostic of anaemia. For children aged 5 to 11 years, haemoglobin below 115g/L is considered diagnostic of anaemia[6].

### Pica

There is another iron-related condition called *pica*. *Pica* is the eating of non-food items and can include things like chalk, clay, foam, cotton wool, anything really. When I have been referred a child for *pica*, I nearly always ask the child's doctor to do a blood test for anaemia. It surprises me how often iron deficiency is missed in cases of *pica*. Even scientific reviews of how to manage *pica* do not recommend considering iron-deficiency as routine[7]. *Pica* is by no means always caused by iron deficiency, but it is tragic when something as "simple" is the case. This is why cases of *pica* should initially be investigated with a blood test for iron deficiency, as it is a common cause of the condition.

## How common is an iron deficiency?

*The National Diet and Nutrition Survey* is a rolling survey in the UK carried out by Public Health England and the Food Standards Agency (I referred to it in the last chapter, when I talked about poor zinc intake). The survey collects information on dietary intake across a random selection of UK households. This diet data is analysed for nutritional intake. Blood and urine samples are also taken for analysis.

The results of the 2008/2009-2011/2012 survey[8] showed that, although the mean (average) haemoglobin concentration was above the lower limit of the normal range in each age and sex group, the proportion of children with a haemoglobin concentration below the lower limits (indicating anaemia) was:

- 12.9% for children aged 1½ to 3 years
- 3.1% for boys aged 4 to 10 years
- 5.7% for girls aged 4 to 10 years

The proportion of children with a ferritin concentration below the lower limit (indicating sub-clinical iron deficiency) was:

- 35.1% for children aged 1½ to 3 years
- 11.1% for boys aged 4 to 10 years
- 20.5% for girls aged 4 to 10 years

Other researchers have estimated that as many as one-third of our toddlers are not getting enough iron in their diets[9]. The rate of iron-deficiency anaemia is the same in some parts of the UK as it is in developing countries[10].

Young children from Asian families seem to be at particular risk[11]. This is probably because these families tend to wean children later, so children drink lots of milk for longer.

## Why is there so much anaemia in the UK?

One reason is, no doubt, excessive milk drinking.

As we learned on Day 7, milk fills young children up, which means they are less hungry for food, and particularly iron-rich food. Dairy products are generally a poor source of iron. The calcium in dairy foods also interferes with how we absorb iron. A second factor is eating too much yoghurt (often sweet children's yoghurts) and/or drinking too much juice.

Finally, I blame our association of a snack with commercial snack foods that are low in iron. I include crisps – in all their permutations! – in this group, as well as biscuits, cereal bars, sweetened yoghurts and other pudding-type foods, cheese and meat "products" (like strings and salami sticks), and fruit-flavoured bars and strings.

Commercial snack foods will have very little in the way of nutrition, other than calories. They are often a poor source of protein, devoid of vitamins, minerals and health-promoting compounds (although some have added vitamins to make them appear healthy), sweetened (whether with sugar or artificially), and made from cheap fats and other undesirable ingredients (or "components", as they are called in the food manufacturing world).

Our reliance on these foods is the result of effective marketing by food manufacturers. Hear the word "snack" and we instantly visualise something pre-packaged.

We have become a nation wedded to the concept of constant grazing, equating snacks with packaged foods. We have forgotten that a snack could be a few slices of apple and a piece of cheese, or half a piece of toast cut into squares topped with cheese spread, butter or nut butter.

## What if I think *my* child is anaemic?

If you suspect that your child might be anaemic then make an appointment to see her doctor, who will probably request a blood test.

If the results show that your child *is* anaemic, then you will probably need a prescribed iron supplement to start with. This will correct the deficiency and build up stores of iron in your child's body.

The doctor will usually recommend another blood test after 3-6 months. Once your child is no longer anaemic, she should be able to get all the iron she needs from her diet.

## Day 9: Try this at home

I have compiled a list of iron-rich foods and meals. For each day of the week, add up how much iron your child is getting.

---

Target: Iron

You will probably need to be aiming, on average, for 3-4 servings each day.

For example:

- ½ beef burger (approx. 1.4mg of iron)
- 1 Weetabix (approx. 2.3mg of iron)
- 2-3 dessertspoons (1 ½ - 2 American tablespoons) baked beans (approx. 0.6mg of iron)
- and 2 dessertspoons (1 ½ American tablespoons) hummus (approx. 0.6mg of iron)

---

Remember that vitamin C helps the body absorb iron from food. It is found mainly in fruits, fruit juices, berries and vegetables (for example, peppers, oranges, strawberries, tomatoes and pure orange juice).

Tea, coffee and fizzy drinks interfere with how we absorb iron from our food, so these – for this reason and many more! – should be avoided for children.

| | Iron | | |
|---|---|---|---|
| | Monday | Tuesday | Wednesday |
| **Red meat**<br>e.g. beef, lamb, liver, pork, kidney, corned beef, beef burgers | | | |
| **Oily fish**<br>e.g. salmon, trout, sardines, pilchards, mackerel (canned or fresh) | | | |
| **Peas, beans and lentils**<br>e.g. baked beans, chickpeas, lentils, mung beans, dhal, tofu, tahini and hummus | | | |
| **Green leafy vegetables**<br>e.g. spinach, cabbage, kale, broccoli | | | |
| **Iron-fortified breakfast cereals**<br>e.g. Weetabix and Ready Brek | | | |
| **Eggs** | | | |
| **Dried fruit**<br>e.g. dried apricots, prunes, currants, sultanas.<br>*These should only be served with a meal, as they can otherwise cause tooth decay.* | | | |
| **Nuts and seeds**<br>*These should be served ground or as butter for children under 5, due to the risk of choking.* | | | |
| **Total** | | | |

| Iron | | | |
|---|---|---|---|
| Thursday | Friday | Saturday | Sunday |
| | | | |
| | | | |
| | | | |
| | | | |
| | | | |
| | | | |
| | | | |
| | | | |
| | | | |

# Day 10: Our Natural Food Preferences

We are now getting to the essence of the programme – moving on to explore how humans learn to like and eat certain foods, and how children learn to like different foods.

Most animals are born instinctively knowing what to eat. Take a lion, for example. Even if it were to be kept in captivity with no contact with other lions, it would never become a vegetarian.

We're a bit different.

Although human babies do get some influence from the tastes that pass through the placenta while in the womb – and some flavours can also pass through breast milk – mostly, humans have to *learn* what is good to eat. We do this through experience, through learning from others and through cultural norms.

## The omnivore's dilemma

Our unusual "suck it and see" method of discovering food preference has left humans in a bit of a pickle.

The issue has been called "the omnivore's dilemma"[1].

By eating a wide range of foods, we are more likely to survive. For example, if winter was very cold and there were fewer edible plants available, we could have survived by hunting more. If a summer drought withered one type of fruit, we could choose from many others.

This omnivorous ability also means humans were able to survive and thrive in many different parts of the world by adapting to the local food sources.

However, we are also born with an inherent mistrust of unfamiliar foods – something we share with far more of the animal kingdom. This wariness has its obvious advantages, too: by sticking to what we know, we're less likely to end up covered in a rash or doubled over with stomach cramps.

This probably explains our natural aversion to bitter taste. Most poisonous plants are bitter, and an aversion to bitter taste might have protected us against poisoning.

### Love & fear

The word neophilia comes from Greek – it means love of the new. Neophobia, also from Greek, means fear of the new.

Because our ancestors were willing to try new foods (food neophilia), while *also* being suspicious of unfamiliar foods (food neophobia), we were more likely to get enough food and nutrition, while avoiding potentially poisonous or toxic plants, animals, and animal products[2].

Researchers think that this dilemma plays a role in explaining why young children can be suspicious of new foods until they have learnt that they are safe to eat[3]. This is particularly the case for toddlers who are just starting to walk and eat a wide range of solid foods[4]. Typically, this suspiciousness of new foods lessens as a toddler grows up.

## Nibble test

Many studies into food aversion have been conducted using rats. This is partly because rats can't vomit, as they lack the required muscles.

Rats also lack any instinct about what to eat and what to avoid, in the same way as humans do. Because they are able to survive on a wide range of different foods, they have to learn what is good to eat and what makes them ill.

Rats do this by taking a small bite of a new kind of food and waiting to see what happens. If the food makes them feel good, they will come back another time and have more of that food. If it makes them ill, they will avoid that food in the future. (This is what makes poisoning rats so hard, a phenomenon known as "bait shyness" – rats soon learn to avoid a poisoned food that makes them ill.)

Plenty of other animal species also take a small bite and wait to see what happens, including many monkeys and even warblers![5]

### Animal instinct

You may have noticed that children often take a tiny nibble of a new food item and wait to see what happens. In fact, many adults do this too.

Humans – adult and children – also study the people around them for clues: "Are they eating it? Do they seem to enjoy it, which means it must be good? Or are they making a disgusted face, which tells me it must be bad?"

We do not know this for sure yet, but some theorise that a small proportion of humans are naturally more sensitive to bitter tastes, and other tastes that might be poisonous, as a way to protect the rest of the group. If this theory is true, then a taste-sensitive person may have had a bite of a new type of food on behalf of a group to see if it tasted OK – and to check whether it might be poisonous.

Of course, it wouldn't be good for *everybody* to be this sensitive, because then we would never try and eat new foods, which might have resulted in us starving.

What does all of this tell us? That some of your child's behaviours around food do have a good reason, even if they might seem odd to you, or odd in a modern world. Don't forget that you already have many years of experience trying and learning about new foods. Your child is just starting on this adventure.

## Our taste and texture preferences

It seems that humans naturally prefer certain flavours and textures over others[6]. We are born with a natural preference for sweet tastes and a dislike, or suspicion, of bitter tastes[7].

## Tastes

Human beings' fondness for sweet-tasting sustenance can be observed in babies straight after birth; even before they have tasted milk*.

This innate preference is probably because a sweet taste indicates a good source of lots of calories[8]. Many years ago, we would have needed those extra calories for energy. Researchers have shown that liking for a type of food can be improved in young children if a new food is served at the same time as a sweet food[9], although I don't recommend you practice this routinely!

We show a preference for fatty foods, too. This is probably for a similar reason – fat is an excellent source of lots of calories that would have been scarce in the past.

We also seem to enjoy the taste of salt from quite early on. This might be because it is essential in small amounts and was hard to come by centuries ago. This isn't the case today, of course, and young children should not have too much salt.

We seem to have an aversion to sour tastes – or at least some of us do. We think that our genes play a role in our preference or aversion to sourness. (Although some might class fruit as sour, most fruits are actually quite sweet. Many parents tell me that their little one enjoys fruit, even if he will not touch a vegetable. This might be because of the sweetness. It might also be because children are usually exposed to fruit in playgroup and nursery, and so copy their peers and learn to enjoy fruit through frequent exposure.)

---

* There are some wonderful black-and-white photographs on the internet from this original research. Newborns were given sweet, sour and bitter tastes straight after birth, before their first milk feed, and their expressions were photographed. Pleased looking baby faces for the sweet taste; and screwed-up faces for the bitter taste!

Children may need longer to learn to like savoury *umami* tastes. Umami is the taste of savoury. It comes from the amino acid glutamate, which is found mainly in protein foods such as meat. Most of us will be familiar with glutamate in the form of monosodium glutamate (MSG) – a flavour additive often associated with soya sauce. It is thought that this taste is learned, rather than instinctual, as protein foods (those containing glutamate) are the most likely to "go off". This may explain why young children are often suspicious of protein foods such as meat, chicken (unless served as chicken nuggets with added sugar or maltodextrin[10]) and eggs. Cheese, even the milder varieties, is either a "love it or hate it" food for young children unless processed (and so made tastier by the manufacturers).

## Textures

We seem to naturally like crispy textures. This might be because "crispy" usually means "fresh".

We often prefer foods that are easy and require little effort to chew. As adults, we see this most commonly in the texture of packaged sandwiches and ready meals – all designed for quick and easy consumption. Young children are no exception, and many picky eaters will devour yoghurts by the carton, especially if it is a sweetened one, but struggle with chewier foods like meat.

## Smells

The nose also plays a role in how we taste food, and in how we remember and learn to like different kinds of food.

This is why smelling a new food item repeatedly can help a young child to dare to have a tiny taste.

## Other factors that play a role in learning to like

Experts have suggested that some people – including children – may be innately pickier than others. There have been various suggestions as to the reason for this disparity.

### In the genes

Some of the difference may be down to genetics[11]. For example, some people may be more "orally sensitive" than others[12]. This means that they may be able to detect tastes and textures more intensely than other people. Many parents tell me that they see distinct food preferences in siblings, and from an early age[13].

### Mental connections

Researchers have discovered that adult picky eaters are more likely to have symptoms of OCD and depression than adults who are not picky eaters[14]. It is, of course, hard to know which came first – whether the symptoms cause picky eating or whether they're a result of it, perhaps because of nutritional deficiencies. One thing we do know is that adults who are picky eaters enjoy eating less – and also eat less healthily – than adults who are not[15].

### Early learning

Some of the differences may be about the surrounding environment and the things that a child has experienced – for example, an illness – during points in his window of "learning to like". We will explore this further in a later chapter but, for now, I just want to say that it doesn't mean that all is lost if a child has missed a critical window; just that it might take a bit longer to learn to like new foods.

Despite genetic differences in our innate taste and texture preferences, much is also learned. Take, for example, research showing that babies who are fed hydrolysed formula (usually used for babies who are intolerant to milk protein) are less likely to be fussy than babies who are fed a normal formula[16].

We think the difference in fussiness is because hydrolysed formulas contain more glutamate, which gives these kinds of milk a very savoury, and even bitter, taste. This research suggests that babies and children can become used to bitter and unusual tastes.

## What can I do to change food preferences?

Despite a natural liking of, or aversion to, certain tastes and textures, most of our food preferences are actually learned. Foods are rarely simple taste sensations (like sweet or bitter), but combinations of tastes, textures, and the other properties of the food that we eat.

Although we might have a natural aversion to bitter tastes, we still enjoy many bitter foods, like beer, olives and coffee.

If you think back to trying these more challenging, bitter flavours for the first time, you will probably remember not liking them to start with. But several exposures and attempts later, you may enjoy them.

I didn't like olives until I was well into my twenties. I still don't like beer today, but that is probably because I haven't persevered enough. I prefer cider, which is easier to like because it is sweeter. I think if I tried beer a few more times, and paired it with tastes I do like, I would probably start to like it.

### How a child can learn to like

A review conducted in 2017 of all the research into how babies and young children learn to like food found four main factors that determine how children learn to like or accept new foods[17]. These are:

1. **Familiarity with a food**

   How familiar a child is with a kind of food means how often he has been exposed to that food, regardless of whether or not he has actually eaten it. This means that just seeing the food on the table or being eaten by others has some effect on a child's liking of it.

2. **Watching and copying role models**
   Children react to their role models' experience and response to a particular food. Role models are mostly parents and other adults involved in mealtimes but can also be siblings and other children.

3. **The consequences of exposure to new foods**
   These consequences can be the child's – such as being sick or vomiting after a food – but more often for young children, the responses are those of other people around him. Young children are masters at picking up cues about whether to try a new food or not by judging the facial expressions of adults and other children.

4. **Categorisation of foods**
   Whether or not a food sits in an expected category, or even whether a new food is thought of as food at all. In psychology, categorisation is the process by which humans place objects, people and anything we come into contact with into one or more categories. For example, "Is it an animal or vegetable?". Some things can be in more than one category.

One example when it comes to food is insects. Do you put this in the category of food or not? My guess is 'not' but, in some cultures, insects belong in the 'food' category.

You will have categorised a good many foods into the 'edible' or 'yummy' category. You will have categorised some foods as 'dessert' and others as 'suitable for breakfast'. Young children are still learning where to put each new food that he comes across.

## Day 10: Try this at home

Think of one or two "challenging" food tastes or textures that you now enjoy.

Challenging tastes and textures might be:

- Beer
- Olives
- Coffee
- Lime pickle
- Caviar
- Smoked salmon

...to mention just a few examples.

How did you learn to like these foods?

Was the food paired with something you already like? This is often how we learn to like coffee, for example. We usually pair it with something sweet to start with. We serve cake or chocolate, or stir in sugar, or make a syrupy coffee or mocha. After a few attempts, many find that they now just like the coffee taste on its own, even without the cake. You might also have first tasted olives with bread or *grissini* or a glass of wine – foods that you already liked. After a few tries, you found that you now just liked olives.

Or you might have been in a social situation where you felt compelled to at least try the new food. You probably weren't too keen the first time around but kept coming across the food in question until one day you realised you now liked it. This is often how we learn to like beer, for example.

If you enjoy a limited range of tastes and textures yourself, talk with a friend or family member, and ask them to describe their experiences of trying new and challenging food tastes and textures.

# Day 11: Learning to Like

As we discussed on Day 10, experts disagree on what proportion of food preference is innate (meaning we are born with it) and how much is what we have learnt to like, mainly as children.

In 2016, researchers published evidence that fussy eating may be genetic. This was reported widely in the press (the BBC, for example, ran the headline *Fussy-eating toddlers 'not the fault of parents'*)[1].

What the research showed[2] when comparing identical twins was that both food fussiness and food neophobia probably have a genetic element.

The research was carried out on 1,932 pairs of twins. Of these, 626 pairs were identical twins and 1,306 were non-identical.

The researchers used the same scale that we used on Day 1 to measure both food fussiness and food neophobia. Food neophobia (from the Greek "fear of new", remember) is thought to be a natural part of toddler development, while food fussiness is not. The researchers used the term food fussiness to mean a child who will eat only a limited variety of foods or a child who refuses many foods.

The researchers found that both food fussiness and food neophobia were significantly correlated in identical twins – if one twin was fussy, the other was likely to be too.

There was a smaller link (correlation) in the non-identical twins – the researchers were less likely to find the same degree of fussiness between non-identical twins.

If environment alone had been causing the food fussiness and/or food neophobia, then twins would show roughly the same degree of fussiness between each pair whether they were identical or non-identical. As there was a difference between the two groups, the authors concluded that at least *some* food fussiness and food neophobia is caused by genetics.

The authors also found that:

> *"the home and familial environment play a more important role in shaping food fussiness than food neophobia in early life."*[3]

This means that food neophobia is more strongly linked to genetics, whereas upbringing played more of a role in food fussiness.

So, what does that mean for my child?

What can we take away from this research to help us understand a child's eating behaviour?

a) Some fussiness is normal for child development.

b) Parents are not to "blame" for fussiness.

c) Even if some fussiness is genetic, there is still lots you can do as a parent to broaden your child's food preferences.

How we respond to toddlers trying or rejecting new or familiar foods helps to shape their future responses to that same food (more on this on Days 21 and 22). The foods that your toddler has seen you eat will also influence her willingness to experiment (more on role modelling on Day 24).

## The science of disgust

Disgust is a core human emotion that exists to protect us from contamination[4].

Humans evolved a sense of disgust as we broadened the range of foods that we ate. This protected us against infection and parasites.

The word 'disgust' literally means 'bad taste'. Disgust is controlled by the part of the brain that is responsible for the perception of taste. It is thought that disgust first evolved in humans as a response to a bad taste in the mouth, presumably indicating food that was off or otherwise not good to eat.

Most of our feelings of disgust are associated with food and anything contaminated entering our mouths[5]. This is why the universal expression of disgust is a screwed up face, closed eyes and stuck-out tongue – it's to try and stop anything from entering our mouths, or to eject whatever is there. Just try it!

Unlike many species, which can stand and walk within a few hours of birth, humans are born quite immature. As babies' brains grow and develop, they learn many of the skills that they will need later in life from those around them. This includes recognising which foods are good to eat, and which may be poisonous or cause contamination.

## Learned aversion

An aversion to a food that has previously made us ill can last a long time, even if we know rationally that the offending foodstuff will not make us ill again.

Ask any woman who was plagued with nausea in pregnancy: even the smell of an offending food is enough to bring on gagging. Food poisoning is another common trigger for food aversion. It can even be something seemingly fleeting; I couldn't eat peanuts for years following an incident of childhood car sickness after sharing a bag of peanuts with my siblings.

Food aversions have also been found to be linked to force-feeding[6]. This is not surprising, given our natural response to avoid food that has previously made us ill. While it can seem like the only solution when faced with a toddler refusing to eat pretty much anything, it invariably backfires. This is why forcing your child to eat something she does not want to eat is never a good idea.

## Cross-contamination

Many parents tell me that their little girl or boy doesn't like foods touching, whether on the plate or even in a sandwich. Parents often find this puzzling, and sometimes annoying.

I usually tell them to simply ignore this behaviour, as it isn't important for the child's nutrition. If parents don't pay attention to this odd habit, it usually disappears (providing your child has plenty of opportunities to see adults and other children happily combining foods).

Still, even if it's not important, it might soothe your frustration to know the background.

It's easy to understand why a child might not like food touching if we look at it from an evolutionary perspective. Research has shown that we will reject food that we know, or think, has been contaminated by something we think of as disgusting.

This is often the case even if the bit we are eating cannot possibly be contaminated[7]. For example, if you saw a cockroach run over one half of your plate and then run off, you wouldn't want to eat the food on the *other* side of the plate, even if you knew that the food on that side of the plate couldn't possibly be contaminated. (Psychology and behavioural researchers actually do this kind of study – usually on psychology students!)

While children younger than 3-5 are not able to think of contamination in such an abstract sense as an adult, considering how we learn what is safe to eat and what is not in these terms might help you to understand some odd toddler food behaviours.

A new food, or a food that she is still unsure about, is a little bit like the side of the plate the cockroach has not been on. Until your little one becomes familiar with and learns to like the new food, all the food on the plate might be contaminated; she might find it just as disgusting as food that has been walked over by a cockroach.

### Copy-cats

Young children learn most of their associations of disgust "culturally". This means that they glean them from watching people around them (and then mirroring them).

Sometimes they get it wrong. For example, when a toddler first starts to learn that poo in the potty is disgusting, she may associate the look of poo with other things that are not usually considered disgusting by adults.

The example I often use with parents is chilli con carne or other browned minced meat dishes. It takes a little more learning to work out that, while poo is disgusting, the smell and look of chilli is something different altogether. It then takes time to get used to the unusual taste.

## Pairing unfamiliar with familiar

As we learned on Day 10, an effective technique for learning to like new foods is pairing a new food with an already liked food[8]. In fact, psychologists have shown that this is a good technique for learning to like lots of new things[9], not only food.

How does this work? Via a mental process that psychologists call "association".

If we pair something new – something that we might be a bit suspicious of – with something we already like, we start to get used to the new thing and associate it with being good (or at least not that bad).

After a few times of this new food (or other thing) just being there, we let our guard down, and then we might try it. It might take a few more tries before we go from, "OK, so it's not going to hurt me," to, "Hmmm, I actually quite like this."

I showed you an example of this in the last chapter when I talked about how adults have to learn to like the taste of coffee. We usually pair coffee with something we already like, usually something sweet. This might be sugar in the coffee, or by pairing coffee with cake or chocolate. Researchers have shown that children can learn to like new flavours and foods in a similar way, by pairing a food that she might be a bit suspicious of with food that she already likes[10].

The researchers who reviewed all of the research into food pairing (we met them at the start of this chapter) disagreed with this advice[11] – possibly because most of the studies compared young children's liking of a new food after 10 paired taste exposures.

We already know that most young children will learn to like a new food after 10 exposures *anyway*, as long as the experience of the new food is positive (meaning she doesn't become unwell or receive a negative response from parents). It would have been more helpful if the research had compared liking after only a few tastes when a new food was paired with an already-liked one, but there we go.

The researchers concluded that more research was needed to understand whether pairing new foods with already-liked foods could help young children to like new foods faster.

In the meantime, you may like to try the following exercise at home.

## Day 11: Try this at home

Place a new food that you would like your child to try on their plate, alongside foods that you know they already like. Don't try and mix the new food item in with other things or allow it to touch other foods if your child doesn't like their foods touching. Place it there and leave it. No pressure, no drama. Don't encourage them to try it.

You should, of course, have some on your plate – make sure you're eating at the same time (role modelling) and visibly enjoying your portion!

When the meal is finished, take away whatever food is left, without comment. Dispose of it and go on to whatever you were going to do next anyway. Don't try and get your child to eat the new food and don't comment on whether the food was eaten or not.

Repeat this for a few meals or snacks until your child starts to mess with it, push it around the plate. Continue enjoying yours. Then, one day, when they try it, give them praise. Researchers have shown that children are more likely to accept new foods if trying them is paired with a positive response[12].

# Day 12: Food Neophobia
# (New Foods from the Perspective of a Toddler)

As very young children start to become more independent and to explore the world on their own, they have more opportunities to eat new foods.

Today, most things a toddler will try to consume will be good to eat – or, at least, not toxic. Many centuries ago, this was quite different. A toddler would have been far more likely to get his hands on things that were poisonous. We think that this explains normal food neophobia in toddlers – that the fear or suspicion of new foods is a clever protective mechanism[1]. It prevents young children, who are exploring the world (and who may, even if just for split seconds, be out of their guardians' sight) from ingesting substances that are potentially harmful.

This suspicion of the new may even extend to familiar and previously enjoyed foods, especially if they are presented in new ways, with unknown foods, or under unfamiliar circumstances.

Plus, as I mentioned in the previous chapter, there may be some genetic differences in food neophobia in young children.

## What's the deal with bitterness?

There are two bitter-tasting compounds that have made news headlines: phenylthiocarbamide and 6-N-propylthiouracil – PTC and PROP for short.

These compounds may explain some food neophobia. Compounds similar to PTC and PROP are found in caffeine, beer, grapefruit juice, saccharine, green tea and dark green vegetables, like brussels sprouts. They give some foods their bitter taste.

However, not everyone can taste PTC, PROP and their related compounds. Whether or not you can taste PTC and PROP is genetically determined. If you are a PROP taster, Brussels sprouts may taste bitter to you, whereas someone else may not be able to taste the bitterness in the same food[2].

### Something in the air

Researchers first discovered these compounds' properties completely by accident. In 1931, scientists were working with PTC in a lab. Some people complained of a bitter taste in the lab – a taste, it turned out, caused by PTC particles in the air. The lead researcher, Arthur Fox, couldn't taste it himself. He started to investigate this variation in people's palates.

Later research concluded that the ability to taste PTC, and a related substance called PROP, was genetic. More recently, scientists have even identified the gene that codes for the ability to taste PTC and PROP.

Researchers divide people into three groups: supertasters, tasters and non-tasters, depending on whether they have one, two, or none of the gene[3]. Supertasters are able to detect very small amounts of PTC and/or PROP, whereas non-tasters are not able to detect it at all.

PTC and PROP made news headlines because the discovery seemed to explain picky and selective eating – supertasters can taste these bitter compounds and reject foods containing them, whereas non-tasters do not[4].

More recently, researchers have found that not all picky and selective eaters are supertasters, so we think that environmental factors, like those I discuss in this book, also play a big part in our food preferences[5].

## How food looks

Research has shown that children respond differently to different aspects of a food's texture and look than adults do.

For example, children seem to prefer a variety of colours, foods that are not mixed together and food with a consistent texture (no lumpy bits!)[6]. Researchers have also found that sensitivity to texture and food pickiness often go hand-in-hand in 1-to-4-year-olds[7]. This is unsurprising when we consider that a young child's instinct is to avoid anything that might be contaminated.

As I said earlier, young children are just learning what is food and what is not food. They are also learning what to avoid so that they don't become ill[8].

Take my chilli con carne example from yesterday. To you and me (as long as you like chilli con carne) the look and smell of a plate of chilli con carne is appealing. You have memories of the taste and you are familiar with the food. You know that it will be tasty.

But, to a young child, a plate of chilli con carne looks very similar to a pile of poo – he is still learning one from the other.

For a young child still learning what is good to eat and what to avoid, things like texture and familiarity matter. Until he is sure of the new food, he is likely to be suspicious of it. Research has shown that young children are universally suspicious of, and will often reject, foods that are covered in sauces, mixed together, brown or multi-coloured[9].

## Contamination

Research conducted by Steven Brown and colleagues at the University of Aberdeen has confirmed what parents of toddlers already know: when a portion of new food is presented alongside a disliked food, and the two foods touch, the disliked food "contaminates" the food that they already like[10]. The children, who were all aged between 4 and 6, were also less likely to try the food that they already liked when it had been in contact with a disliked food.

So, if your little one doesn't like his food touching, don't serve new foods touching others on the plate – it is quite likely that he will then reject food that was previously considered to be OK.

## Day 12: Try this at home

List three foods that your child has been offered but will not eat. Think of the context of when your child refused this food, and your response to their food refusal. Finally, try and think about the situation from the perspective of your toddler. I have filled in an example.

| | Food type | What was happening at the time? |
|---|---|---|
| *Example* | *Carrots* | *Emily eats her dinner with her older brother. He was also messing around, saying they were disgusting.* |
| Food 1 | | |
| Food 2 | | |
| Food 3 | | |

| How did I respond? | How does this sound from my toddler's perspective? |
|---|---|
| *I told Harry to stop being silly and eat the carrots because they were good for him. Emily still wouldn't eat hers, so I told her that if she ate them, she could have ice-cream for pudding.* | *Being told that carrots are good for you probably didn't wash with either of them, and the reward let the kids know that I also don't think carrots are nice.* |
| | |
| | |
| | |

# Day 13: Exposure

So far, we have talked about how our genes help shape our food preferences (which we can't change); and about how we learn to prefer and like certain foods (which we *can* change).

## Behaviour = learned response

Things about us that are shaped by experience and environment can be loosely grouped in a category called "behaviours". So, the techniques used to improve the liking of new foods are commonly called "behavioural strategies".

Parents are sometimes (understandably) upset by this term because they think it means their child has a problem with her behaviour, that they have not been good parents or that they are being judged as parents.

However, what we mean by behaviour in this context is a learned response to our environment.

A non-food example of a learned (behavioural) response is when we quickly move our hand away from a very hot source. We would call this a behavioural response (because we learnt to do it after burning ourselves), without meaning that our parents were in some way negligent.

## Strategies

The three main behavioural strategies that are shown to be effective in increasing the variety of foods that young children eat are:

1. Exposure
2. Role modelling
3. Positive reinforcement of desirable behaviour (such as attention) and not reinforcing behaviour that we don't want to see more of (such as giving them attention, whether this is good attention or scolding/ telling off)[1]

Today, I am going to focus on number 1: exposure. I have talked about exposure a little bit over the last few days of this programme – but we didn't go into any great detail.

## Food exposure – the research

What we know from research is that exposure to a new type of food makes children more likely to become familiar with it and, therefore, to like it[2].

How does exposure work?

Exposure actually *changes* the part of the brain that is responsible for the perception of taste[3]: the gustatory cortex.

Studies in rats show that these brain changes take 24 hours to show up after exposure to the new food.

### Keep trying

The number of exposure attempts varies somewhat by study, but most have used ten[4].

This means that broadly speaking, you should expect to try your child with a new sort of food at least ten times before concluding that she doesn't like the food. Even then, it may still be an idea to offer a rejected food from time to time – and to role model it as a positive experience by having some yourself.

Most of the studies into exposure only exposed children to a new food item ten times before the study stopped. It is quite probable that, had researchers continued and exposed children to the new food 20 or 30 times, even more of the children in the studies would have accepted the new food.

For example, in a study conducted by the late Professor Jane Wardle and colleagues at University College London[5], 49 children aged between

5 years, 8 months old and 7 years, 10 months old were assessed for their liking for, and consumption of, pieces of red pepper. The assessment was done before and after exposure to red pepper every day for 10 days.

Liking was assessed using a five-point 'faces' scale (scored 2 to -2) designed to represent the following responses:

- 'I like it a lot'
- 'I like it a little bit'
- 'It is okay'
- 'I dislike it a little bit'
- 'I dislike it a lot'

The children in the exposure group went from an average of -0.06 (somewhere between 'It is OK' to 'I dislike it a little bit') to an average score of 2 ('I like it a lot').

What is perhaps more interesting is that the children went from consuming two pieces of red pepper on Day 1 to consuming nine pieces by Day 10. The graph showing how much red pepper the children consumed goes up and up each day.

Who knows – if the study had continued for another 10 days then the graph's line may have carried on climbing.

Another example of the importance of repeated exposure was cleverly demonstrated by a group of researchers in Dijon, France in 2013[6].

Some 95 infants were fed an artichoke puree (of all things!). The researchers wanted to see which method was the most effective for increasing these infants' liking and acceptance of the unique taste.

The researchers found that repeatedly offering artichoke puree to the infants two to three times per week increased their liking of artichoke puree by 21%, and the amount the infants would eat by 63%.

This was more effective than sweetening the artichoke puree, which didn't increase their liking at all.

By the end of the study, the 95 infants liked artichoke puree as much as they liked carrot puree (which is quite sweet and liked by most babies).

Interestingly, the researchers also reported that how much artichoke puree a baby would eat before the study started was related to how many vegetables she had already been exposed to. It seems that the more foods a young child already eats, the more willing she is to accept new foods. This effect may even last into adulthood – if we eat something often in childhood, it is quite probable that we will like the same food as an adult[7].

## Long-term benefits

Most studies continued to monitor the children' acceptance of the new food after the exposure period. The researchers concluded that children liked the new food long after the exposure period ended.

This seems to mean that, once a child has accepted a new food into her diet, the food will stay in her diet. Of course, she may still test the boundaries, and your reaction, by refusing it from time to time. Ignore this behaviour. And don't forget that an accepted food, presented in a completely new way, may seem like a completely new food to your toddler.

To summarise, we know that exposure and liking of one food can increase a child's liking for similar foods[8]. This is the principle behind "food chaining", which we will look at more on Day 27. Exposure seems to be incremental: the more new foods a young child is exposed to, the more likely she is to accept other new foods[9].

### Familiarity rules...

Research has shown that getting used to something new through repeated exposure helps us to become familiar with the new thing, or experience.

The effect of exposure is powerful. It even works just by having the food in sight on the table[10]. Just seeing *pictures* of unfamiliar foods can increase a child's willingness to try new food[11].

As well as preferring the taste of familiar foods, we also like smells that we are familiar with.

### ...but don't forget the variety

On the other hand, we can also go off food if we eat it lots of times, at least for a short while[12].

*'We had curry yesterday so we don't want it again today…
but by next week we'd love some!'*

This highlights why it is so important to increase the variety of foods that your child will eat – I have seen many children eat an ever-narrower range of foods as they become fed up with old favourites.

Most were able to eat a greater range of foods when applying the techniques in this book.

## Actionable steps

What does all of this mean for parents?

Try increasing your child's familiarity with new (or refused) foods in steps, and don't give up first (or second, or third) time around.

The consensus in the scientific community is that it might take a child as many as 15 attempts at trying a new food for her to start to like it[13].

Start by letting your little one see a new food first. This could be on her plate (remember: 'you don't have to eat it'), on your plate and/or on serving plates in the middle of the table.

Let her see the new food a few times. Eat it and enjoy it yourself. Have a few days' break. Then serve it up again, eat it and enjoy it yourself. Repeat. This will get your child used to seeing and smelling the food.

You might then ask if she would like a taste on her plate when you dish up (if she hasn't already asked for some). Only do this if you can do it without pressure. Leave it for a few days, then try serving it up again.

### Dual-purpose

Don't forget that the techniques discussed in this chapter and in the rest of this book that help increase your child's acceptance of *tastes* also work for increasing your child's acceptance of *textures.*

Exposing your child to new foods presented in different textures helps increase acceptance of different textures generally, as well as the new taste[14]. We will look at this in more detail on Day 27.

## Day 13: Try this at home

Try offering a familiar food alongside a new or less familiar food.

For some children, it will be enough to offer new foods alongside already-liked foods a few times. This will increase their liking for the new food.

For others, a more structured approach may be needed. If this is the case, try introducing new food to your child step-by-step (see below). This way, they get to feel proud of achieving something despite their fear. You get the chance to give lots of attention and praise, even if they haven't managed to try the new food. This praise also lets your child feel good about themselves.

Remember, it is really important that you do not pressure your child or expect them to go faster than their own pace.

1. Have a new food in the same room as your child.
2. Have the new food on the table for a meal, without expecting that they try it. If your child is particularly anxious, it might help if the food is a little way away from them.
3. Move the food in its serving bowl a little closer to your child at the table.
4. Ask your child to just smell the food and demonstrate this yourself. Make sure you keep a positive and smiling face – they will pick up on your cues.
5. Let your child touch the food with a spoon or fork (not with their hands).
6. Let your child touch the food through something floppier, like a napkin or tissue. There is more chance of accidentally touching the food, so this might be harder. They will get more of a feel for the shape and texture of the food through a napkin or tissue.
7. Let your child touch the food, by handing it to somebody else.
8. Have the new food in a bowl separate from their main plate.
9. Have the new food on the same plate as their meal, but away from already-liked foods. Remember, you are not expecting them to try the food yet unless they do so of their own accord.
10. Let your child kiss the food. Demonstrate this yourself, keeping a positive and smiling face.
11. Let your child lick the food. As above, demonstrate this and keep positive and happy.
12. Let your child put a tiny piece of the new food in their mouth and take it out again. Re-assure your child that they don't have to swallow it, just put it in their mouth and take it out again (but without spitting it out). Demonstrate this.

13. Let your child take a tiny bite and chew it. Tell your child that if they really cannot swallow it, they can spit it into a napkin. You might have to show your child how to do this first. Remember to give lots of praise for just doing this step.
14. Finally, let your child take a tiny bite, chew and swallow. You are only expecting one tiny bite, and then they can leave the rest. Give lots of praise if they manage this. If not, just shrug and say not to worry, you can try again another day. Take one tiny taste yourself, staying upbeat and positive and making lots of fuss about how yummy it is.

If your child wants to skip steps and move right on, then go for it – let them go as far as they are comfortable with and remember to give them lots of praise for doing so.

# Day 14: Repeated Exposure

Yesterday we looked at how repeated exposure (without pressure) is key for allowing young children to learn to like new foods.

In fact, repeated exposure without negative consequences is a key tool to get *anybody* to like *anything*. Humans can be suspicious and wary of unfamiliar situations. The more often we are exposed to the new thing or situation, the more familiar it becomes.

The more we see and experience new foods, the more we like them[1]. It seems that the combination of exposure, followed by pleasure from the food or from feeling full, makes a child realise that the new food is safe to eat[2].

## Conditioning

Learning to associate certain situations with a positive or negative response is called 'conditioning' in psychology.

If we have learnt to associate a situation or experience with a positive response, we are likely to want to repeat that experience. If we have learnt to associate a situation with a negative response, we learn to avoid the situation.

It is possible to unlearn a negative association, but much harder than starting with no association.

Once a young child has learnt that something is disgusting or undesirable, unlearning this association is often much harder than starting from scratch. For this reason, I often recommend that parents do not introduce new foods with people who are going to teach the child that this food is disgusting (for example, with his teenage cousin who might make a drama about any piece of vegetable on the plate). Once a dislike is learned, it is much harder to unlearn.

## Keep trying

Research has shown that one of the key methods for getting young children to learn to like new foods, tastes and textures is to expose them to the food many times[3]. It is even effective for children on the autistic spectrum.

But most parents give up after a few times, concluding that their child does not like this or that food. Research has shown that, on average, parents give up after trying a new food between 3 and 5 times[4].

This is completely understandable, as it is heartbreaking to put time and effort into preparing food for your family or child, only to have the meal or food rejected. Never mind the expense, and throwing food away.

It's also another reason why I am a great advocate of family meals wherever possible. It is less stressful and worrying if at least some family members will eat the food you have prepared, even if one or two refuse it.

Although this sounds simple, it is incredibly difficult for parents.

For one thing, it means that the whole family has to eat the same food and meal. But, when everybody is eating the same thing, it doesn't matter quite so much when one member of the family turns down part or all of the meal. The waste is not so great and the rejection less acute.

The second difficulty with this approach is that it places a demand on you, too, to try new foods – foods that *you* may not have yet learned to like. But only by eating the same food as your child will he see the most important role model in his life – you – enjoy the food you are expecting him to eat.

You may be feeling a little anxious about the pressure of this process yourself. Keep trying. This is a voyage of discovery for everybody that can only end in one place – a greater variety of food eaten and enjoyed by the whole family, and less stressful mealtimes.

The message of Day 14 of 'Help! My Toddler Is Not Eating' is simple: Keep trying. Keep offering different foods again and again and on many occasions.

## Exposure without pressure

As I mentioned yesterday, repeated exposure can work even if the child just *sees* the food without any pressure to eat it. In fact, removing the pressure to eat can help, by reducing anxiety associated with the new food. This is particularly true for children who already have food-related anxiety issues.

One of the really, really, *really* important parts of repeated exposure is for it to be done without pressure. Research (again!) has shown that young children are less likely to eat a particular food, or any food, if they are put under pressure to eat.

### The Tiny Tastes technique

There are several techniques for repeated exposure. One of these techniques is called 'Tiny Tastes'. The principle of this method is to encourage young children to take just an itsy taste of a new food without pressure to eat it. It is thought that taking just a tiny taste, even without swallowing, gets a child used to this new type of food.

The 'Tiny Tastes' method adds an additional step beyond simple exposure for particularly neophobic toddlers: external rewards. The method offers children a sticker in exchange for taking the tiny taste.

The technique was developed by Dr Lucy Cooke, a psychologist in London who specialises in child feeding. She led a research project (also called Tiny Tastes), which was shown to be very successful at encouraging young children who were picky eaters to try just one little bite.

The child and parent try a morsel of a new food every day for 15 days. The child doesn't have to swallow the food, nor eat any more – just one small taste. If she manages it, then she gets a sticker on a sticker chart.

As we have covered, if a young child tries a new food several times, she will often start to like it. The 'tiny taste' is less overwhelming than a full portion, and there is no pressure for the child to eat any more, nor to actually swallow the food if she really can't – it's OK for her to spit it out.

The method also uses what is called 'extrinsic rewards'. An extrinsic reward is something that you get in exchange for doing something. In contrast, 'intrinsic rewards' are a sense of achievement from inside yourself.

**Reward controversy**

Many people in the child feeding world disagree with rewards of *any* description in exchange for eating or trying new foods; including my hero, Ellyn Satter[5]. This is because research has shown that external rewards (like stickers for children, or money for adults) can reduce our internal motivation to want to do something without the reward.

Those who oppose external rewards for a behaviour argue that rewards will make children less likely to continue a behaviour without recompense. They also say that it teaches a child that the food is less desirable – after all, why else would you give them a reward?

Despite this, we used a version of Tiny Tastes in a healthy family living programme that I developed in Wales. In the evaluation at the end of the programme, parents told us that they felt this part of the programme was one of the most useful techniques for encouraging their children to eat a better variety of foods.

## Day 14: Try this at home

I'm still deciding where I sit in this debate – I can see the arguments both for and against. For now, I feel that no book about food refusal in young children would be complete without including a practice that you can use at home.

My advice, for now, is to save this technique and use it as a last resort.

**Tiny Tastes food exposure technique:**

1. Choose a vegetable that you would like your child to eat (and that you usually have in the house).
2. Tell your child that you are going to play a tasting game at snack-time (or when they are moderately hungry).
3. Show your child the whole vegetable, name it and say that you are both going to have a tiny taste of it.
4. Cut a very small piece for yourself and a similar one for your child.
5. Try your piece and say how delicious it is.
6. Ask your child to try their piece. Tell them that they can spit it out if they really don't like it.
7. Give your child a sticker on their sticker chart for tasting their piece, even if they spit it out.
8. Repeat with the same vegetable every day for at least 10 days, up to 15 days.
9. Choose another vegetable and start again.

*Adapted from Weight Concern*

You can buy 'Tiny Tastes' packs, complete with full instructions and sticker charts, from the Weightconcern website: *bit.ly/FussyDay14*.

**Disclaimer**: I have no association with this website, nor 'Tiny Tastes', and do not profit in any way if you purchase a pack. My only interest is to encourage researchers to develop techniques that help parents encourage their children to eat as wide a range of foods as possible!

# Day 15: Pressure to Eat

Young children don't eat well under pressure.

It may be because it raises the expectations that are placed on them.

It may be because their parents' anxiety over food and eating becomes an opportunity for children to exert some control over their parents, or over their environment more generally; an environment which they otherwise have little control over.

It may be a more basic human survival instinct. Anxiety when eating tells the body that something's amiss in the environment; or even that this food may be contaminated or not good to eat.

## Force is *forbidden*

Whatever you do, and however much or little of the advice in this book you follow, promise me to never, ever force a child to eat.

Forcing a child to eat will not improve his eating and can leave a lasting, negative impression of eating and mealtime behaviour.

I once met a 12-year-old girl, referred for a suspected eating disorder. Fortunately for her (and her parents), she did not have an eating disorder. She 'just' had a very fussy eating pattern that was limiting her intake, had made her anaemic and made mealtimes a battle.

During this girl's assessment, she could vividly recount an episode when her grandmother had force-fed her as a toddler. It only happened once, but she could still remember it clearly. Her parents thought this incident was behind her eating problems all these years later.

I am not saying that, if you have crossed this line already, all is lost. If you struggle from this point forward keeping your cool at mealtimes, seek help. You can't make your child eat, so give up the battle.

## Bribing backfires

Pressure to eat has been consistently found by researchers to make a child eat less[1]. Worse, forcing a child to eat something can put him off that food for life[2].

A systematic review of the factors related to picky eating in young children, conducted in 2017, found a clear link between offering rewards for eating and fussy eating habits[3]. (A systematic review looks at all research papers published on a topic and goes to great lengths to make sure that none are missed out.)

The reviewers also found a clear relationship between pressure to eat and fussy eating. Children who are pressured to eat more – whether bribed, cajoled, begged or coaxed – actually eat less. Another 2017 review also found that pressure to eat reduces intake[4].

Pressure just doesn't work.

Today, I will focus on *why* these tactics, employed by desperate parents in an attempt to get their little ones to eat just a little more, don't work.

But before I explore these issues, I'd like us to stop, just for a moment, and consider the expression to eat "just one more bite".

## "Just one more bite"

Feeding and nurturing our children is one of the most basic human desires. A parent's wish to get their child to eat a little more is quite deep-rooted. It served a purpose in times when food was scarce, and we were unsure of the nutritional value of the next meal.

Things are different today. Most of us can feel confident that we will be able to provide enough calories at our son or daughter's next meal, so encouraging young children to eat more at this particular meal is far less important. It is, like so many human survival habits, largely redundant.

Today, we are probably best off leaving a child to learn to eat according to his appetite. By that, I mean allowing him to tune in to how much food he needs at a meal – and to stop eating when this need has been met.

Research has shown that children who are not allowed to listen to their full-up signals are more likely to be either picky eaters or overweight.

Most adults do not know that young children can regulate their energy intake very well, getting just as much as they need[5]. This knowledge gap is not surprising, as adults are unduly influenced by portion sizes, package sizing, social expectations and so forth; rather than listening to our own bodies' cues and signals.

A young child will happily leave one bite of a piece of toast, claiming to be 'full up'; whereas an adult will usually finish the piece of toast, even if he is full. Teach your child to respect his satiety signals by not encouraging him to eat "just one more bite".

## Let children eat as much as they need

Ellyn Satter uses the term "the division of responsibility" in her book '*Child of Mine: Feeding with Love and Good Sense*'[6] to describe when parents should be in charge at mealtimes, and when children should take the reins.

She recommends that:

1. Parents decide, "what, when and where" food is eaten
2. Children decide, "if, and how much" they will eat

This method allows children to learn to eat perfectly according to their nutritional needs. On Day 3, we looked at how otherwise healthy children are generally very good at growing – this includes eating enough calories to meet their growth needs.

### What does this mean for parents?

Mainly that you don't need to get your child to eat just a bit more, or to finish his plate. As parents, 'all' you need to do is to present the food that you wish him to eat, in a serving size that is realistic for his age, in a relaxed, social atmosphere with role models around. Then sit back and enjoy your own food.

Now, I know this sounds very easy in writing, and much harder in practice. But the principle is to not worry too much if he fusses or won't touch the carrots today. To not worry if he eats only a few bites from each food, before declaring that he is full, or otherwise had enough. That's fine.

You are not going to offer any alternatives (more on this later in the programme). Nor are you going to offer pudding/dessert contingent on him finishing what is on his plate. You're just going to say, 'well done', and finish your own food (or, rather, eat until you are comfortably satisfied). No stress.

## "Finish your soup"

And what about cajoling, begging and coaxing? As we've discussed, research has highlighted these methods as really *very* ineffective at getting young children to eat more. It just puts them off.

This was cleverly demonstrated by researchers in a research paper called '*"Finish your soup": counterproductive effects of pressuring children to eat.*'[7].

Children were split into two groups and offered identical soup for lunch. The first group was allowed to eat as much or as little of the soup as they wanted. The second group was coaxed and cajoled into finishing their soup.

At the end of the meal, both groups were asked how much they liked the soup. The group that had been coaxed and cajoled liked the soup less than the group that had been allowed to eat as much or as little as they wanted.

I wonder what the children in the second group would say if they were offered the same soup again!

## Accidental aversions

Forcing a child to eat food that he is averse to might cause a long-lasting food aversion[8]. Many long-term food dislikes can be traced back to an event when a child was forced to eat something.

Yes, he can still learn to love, or at least like, a particular food, using the strategies in this book. But right now, if he really is averse to a particular food, then the best strategy is for him to watch you (and other adults and children) eat and enjoy that food. Hopefully, he will then want to copy you; and he will be praised for doing so.

## Portion control

Later on, we will look at portion sizes in more detail. For now, let me just say that you should offer your child smaller portion sizes, so as not to overwhelm him.

Young children need to feel they are achieving, and you must, therefore, make it possible for him to achieve finishing some or most of his food at mealtimes. Giving him larger portions in an attempt to 'get' him to eat more than appetite dictates is likely to backfire.

This means trusting his appetite and allowing him to decide when he has had enough. Trust your child's appetite to eat just the right amount for him, at that particular meal.

## Offer no alternatives

Don't offer alternatives, even if you feel that your child hasn't eaten enough. Alternatives will not only undo all of the good work and effort you have put in so far, but they will also almost always be less healthy than the food you originally offered.

Leanne Birch, a professor of psychology at the University of Georgia, did much of the early work studying children's eating behaviour. She, like many others after her, found that children eat less well at subsequent meals if there is pressure to eat in any way. This includes special meals being prepared just for your child.

You have probably already noticed that the more effort you go to, the less well your child eats – including when you offer replacements for refused food.

Birch's research found that children eat best when they are left to eat at their own pace. Interestingly, the research also found there was one factor that parents can influence and that improves how well a child eats: the presence of a trusted adult. So, eat with your child, whenever you can.

## Parental anxiety

Studies have shown that if parents are anxious around mealtimes, a child is more likely to be fussy with food[9].

A team of researchers examined how pressure to eat at mealtimes affects food fussiness and weight-for-height in 222 young children[10]. Parents were asked to complete questionnaires on three separate occasions: the first when their child was 21 months old, the second at 27 months old, and the last when they were 33 months old. The children were also weighed and measured.

Although the researchers were not able to show that pressure to eat made the children fussier, they *did* show that pressure to eat had no effect on the children's weight-for-height. In other words, no amount of pressure to eat will make your child eat more and gain weight.

## Day 15: Try this at home

The researchers mentioned above used two different questionnaires to assess the children's eating habits, and one to assess how parents fed their children.

The questionnaire used to assess how parents fed their child was developed by researchers at the University of North Carolina. It is called the *Infant Feeding Style Questionnaire (IFSQ)*. The Infant Feeding Style Questionnaire (IFSQ) has a subsection called 'Pressure to Finish'.

For today's home practice, I am going to ask you to complete this part of the questionnaire. It might be helpful if any other family members involved in your child's meals and snacks also have a go. This questionnaire is also very helpful if parents, or grandparents, disagree on feeding practices.

Many parents find that just answering the questions is very revealing.

You will probably find that questions 1 and 8 are no longer relevant to you.

For each question, pick where you sit on a scale of 1-5 by circling the number that best reflects how you feel and what you think, where:

1 = Never

2 = Rarely

3 = Sometimes

4 = Often

5 = Always

| Question | My score |
|---|---|
| It's important that an infant finish all of the milk in his or her bottle. | 1 2 3 4 5 |
| It's very important that a toddler finish all the food that is on his or her plate. | 1 2 3 4 5 |
| I try to get (name of child) to eat even if s/he seems not hungry. | 1 2 3 4 5 |
| If (name of child) will not try a new food that I give him/her, I will work hard to have him/her try it during that meal. | 1 2 3 4 5 |
| I praise (name of child) after each bite to encourage him/her to finish his/her food. | 1 2 3 4 5 |
| I try to get (name of child) to finish his/her food. | 1 2 3 4 5 |
| If (name of child) seems full, I encourage him/her to finish his/her food anyway. | 1 2 3 4 5 |
| I try to get (name of child) to finish his/her milk. | 1 2 3 4 5 |

What came up for you after you finished this exercise?

**Try this at home - extra credit!**

You are now halfway through 'Help! My Toddler Is Not Eating'. This is a good time for a quick check-in to see how far you have come. Go online to my website (*fussyaboutfood.com/survey*) and complete, for the second time, the subsections of the Child Eating Behaviour Questionnaire (CEBQ) that you did at the beginning of the programme. As before, if you are prompted for a code, then use *BOOK20*.

Once you have finished the programme (and completed the questionnaire three times throughout the programme), I will send you your results.

*If you enjoyed working through this book so far, and have seen positive changes, I would be very grateful if you could leave an honest review on Amazon or wherever you bought your copy. This will help other parents find this book in the maze of others out there. If you would like to recommend changes or additions for the next edition, then please get in touch through my website fussyaboutfood.com/contact.*

# Day 16: Reducing Mealtime Anxiety

Fear of new foods is the cause of mealtime anxiety in some children, especially if they have had a negative experience with the food in the past.

There are several ways of reducing the anxiety that your toddler may be experiencing around a particular food. We have already explored some of these strategies in earlier chapters: increasing familiarity without pressure to eat it; and positive feedback for any interaction with the food.

These strategies are enough for most picky eaters but, for some, a little more work is needed. It may even be that the "usual" strategies have worked well for most foods, but there are still a few which your toddler is wary of.

It is, of course, not necessary for your child to eat absolutely *every* food that the adults enjoy. Given time, she will probably learn to enjoy a greater variety of foods on her own.

But, for children who are a little more resistant to trying new foods, there are few more things to try.

One technique, which we covered on Day 13, is increasing familiarity with the food without the need to try it, within the context of the mealtime. This includes techniques such as having the food in the same room as your child, just having the food on the table for a meal and touching the food with a spoon or fork.

The second strategy is increasing a child's familiarity with new foods outside of a kitchen or dining context. This means, mainly, what is called "messy play".

## Messy play and safe prep

Naturally, some foods lend themselves better to messy play and other activities than others.

It is easy, for example, to paint with jam or build a house with fish fingers. It's a bit harder to think of a way to play with chilli con carne!

Nevertheless, it is possible. For example, you could *build* a chilli with dried kidney beans and brown playdoh, adding dried rice for effect (always under adult supervision). You could even make a side salad using green paper, with red and green cardboard circles for tomato and cucumber.

I will explore messy play in more detail during Day 17's 'Try it at home' exercise.

Once your child is comfortable with the food outside of the mealtime, you could introduce the food at mealtime, without the pressure to try it.

Depending on her age and abilities, the best way to do this is by having her help you at mealtimes. You can get special, safe-to-use, child-friendly cutlery like the Kuhn Rikon Kinderkitchen Children's Dog Knife. With child-friendly cutlery, young children can 'help out' by chopping ingredients for the meal or table.

I have run programmes with ten little tots in their chefs' hats and aprons, happily 'chopping' away at tomatoes for their own individual pizzas.

## Sensory processing issues

For young children with sensory processing issues, it can help to identify environmental triggers of anxiety or stimulation, as well as the environmental factors that reduce anxiety and stimulation. These can include lighting, noise and other distractions.

Some children with sensory processing issues may find different types of sensory input overwhelming (referred to as hypersensitive, or over-sensitive). Reducing their sensory input can help the child get to the calmer mindset needed to focus on food.

*Hypo*sensitive, or under-sensitive, children may need and seek out additional sensory input. For these children, providing that extra sensory input will usually help at mealtimes.

We have, as you know, several senses. They include hearing, sight, touch, taste, smell, vestibular and proprioception. Most will be familiar with the first five.

Our **vestibular** sense is our sense of balance and spatial orientation. This is most familiar in the context of travel sickness – the eyes tell the brain it is in one place, while the inner ears sense something different. This can confuse the brain, which leads to motion sickness.

**Proprioception** is our sense of where our body is located in space and in relation to other objects, and how the different parts of our body are moving.

## Adjusting the volume

A child with sensory processing issues may need "the volume" turning down or up in one or more of these senses to achieve a calmer state.

- If a child needs less stimulation (the volume turned down) in one or more sensory domains, then she is said to be over-responsive in that sensory domain.
- If a child needs additional input (the volume turned up) in one or more sensory domains, then she is said to be under-responsive in that sensory domain.

For example, a child that is over-responsive to sound might perceive it more acutely than you and I. For that child, making sure that mealtimes are quiet is important. If they are loud, it could heighten her unease.

School or nursery dining rooms might just be too much for this child, leading to anxiety and poor dietary intake.

Another child might be hyposensitive to one or more of these senses – so additional stimulation may help her to become calm. If a child is hyporesponsive to proprioceptive (the space/movement sense) stimulation, for example, then additional proprioceptive stimulation before a meal may help her to come to the table in a calmer state. This can be as simple as draping a heavy blanket over the child's shoulders and back. It is thought that the proprioceptive stimulation created by a heavy blanket (or a weighted blanket) simulates deep pressure stimulation. Deep pressure stimulation has been found to calm some adults and children with anxiety, autism and attention difficulties[1].

## Day 16: Try this at home

I have listed six different types of sensory stimulation we get from our environment (I have taken these categories from research done by Silje Steinsbekk and her team in 2017[2]).

For each type, select whether your child is sensitive or not.

Add up the answers. If your child scores more than 1 or 2 in the "yes" column, you may benefit from seeking the help and advice of an occupational therapist.

| | My child is sensitive *(gets upset or tries to run away)* | |
|---|---|---|
| Type of stimulus | Yes | No |
| **Tactile (touch)**<br>Sensitive to clothes, fabrics, tags, seams, etc.? | | |
| **Oral (of the mouth)**<br>Sensitive to crisp, hard or soft textures? | | |
| **Taste**<br>Sensitive to sour, bitter, sweet, salty or very savoury tastes? | | |
| **Smell**<br>Sensitive to perfume, fragrances, cooking smells, etc.? | | |
| **Sound**<br>Sensitive to sharp or loud sounds, areas with lots of different sounds? | | |
| **Visual**<br>Sensitive to bright sunlight or other lights? | | |
| **Total:** | | |

# Day 17: Children with Food-Related Anxiety or Phobia

For some children, trying new food is just too much.

This might be because your child is particularly wary of new foods, or because of previous bad experiences. Whatever the reason, trying certain foods or new foods might just be a step too far. Any pressure to try the food raises anxiety even further.

For these children, exposure without actually *eating* the food can help. This technique is sometimes called 'messy play' – we looked at it briefly in the last chapter – and is often used for children with sensory processing issues. More on this in today's exercise!

By handling food, and becoming more familiar with a food's sensory properties, a child can better anticipate how this food will feel in her mouth. She may then be less apprehensive about the new food and more likely to try it.

## Cook's treat

Food exposure without the pressure to eat can be more than just messy play. Some children respond well to baking or making food, without the expectation that she will eat what is made. She may like to help with mealtime activities:

- Stirring or mixing foods
- Drizzling sauces and dressings
- Sprinkling or sieving an ingredient
- Arranging food on a plate

Your child might enjoy giving away the food or cake she has made and watching others eat it. She may even be encouraged, when she sees others enjoying the food, to take a tiny bite.

It is really important that this is not forced or rushed – let your child go at her own pace. If she wants to try, then great! Give her lots of attention and praise. If she isn't ready for that quite yet, never mind, no disappointment, maybe next time.

Try not to go into this *expecting* your child to try the food, as she will pick up on the anticipation and feel pressured – probably making her more reluctant, not less. It may also make her less likely to want to play with food another time.

If food prep is too much for your child's age or confidence – or if it is proving too stimulating for a child with sensory processing issues – she might be able to help with setting or laying the table, carrying bowls to the table and helping to clear up after a meal.

## More activities to try

Other ways of exposing your child to new foods include:

- Taking her food shopping and letting her help by choosing foods and putting them in the trolley or basket.
- Looking at, and perhaps collecting, food pictures – in a magazine, a book, or online.
- Your child might be able to help you pick out a recipe to make for the whole family or others, even if she is not expected to actually try any of the food.
- Try one or more of the wonderful food stories and food storybooks for young children.
- Naming foods (showing a picture of a food, or the actual food, and having your child guess the name) has been shown to help make young children more accepting of a new type of food[1]. It seems to help young children identify new food and put it into the category of 'good to eat'.

### No pressure!

This bears repeating. Whatever you do, don't force or cajole your child to eat. Research has shown that forcing a child to eat when they are feeling disgust toward a food (mainly because the food is unfamiliar) can lead to a long-lasting food aversion[2].

## Day 17: Try this at home

Today I have included two exercises instead of the usual one.

They are both fun exercises to do together, so I hope you enjoy them both!

### Exercise 1: Getting stuck in with messy play

A technique that works for many children with food phobias is getting them used to handling food without having to eat it. This can be done through play.

Some fun games include:

| Game idea | How you played it/how it went |
|---|---|
| Creating a picture with spaghetti shapes, lentils or couscous | |
| Making shapes out of fruits and vegetables and use these as stamps with paint | |
| Painting with yoghurt or custard<br>*With a paintbrush or fingers!* | |
| Making potato (or another vegetable) men or heads | |
| Sort foods into different shapes, or different colours<br>*Great for children who like sorting and ordering* | |
| Cutting out food shapes<br>*You could use cookie cutters with dough, slices of bread, cheese, or harder fruit and vegetables such as melon, potato and swede* | |
| Make simpler shapes with food<br>*e.g. squares of cheese or bread, or balls of melon* | |

If your child is sensitive to the feel of food on their fingers, be sure to have some wipes or plenty of kitchen roll handy.

**Exercise 2: Getting used to food with the help of pictures**

Research has shown that seeing pictures of unfamiliar foods can increase a child's willingness to try them[3]. It seems to be particularly helpful if the pictures are accompanied by a story about where the food came from, how it was made, and so forth[4].

This exercise is all about having fun with your child with food pictures.

Go online and choose 5-10 pictures of food that you can colour in with your child. I have found that typing the words "food pictures to colour" straight into Google works well.

Print out a couple of copies of each picture (or more, if there are siblings or other adults who want to join in). Depending on your child's attention span, you could work on just one or two each day.

You might want to start with a picture of a food that your child already likes, before moving on to new and unfamiliar foods. Then, mix pictures of foods that your child already likes with pictures of new foods.

Give lots of praise for how well coloured in each picture is, the nice colours they used, etc.

If you are going to use a picture of a kind of food they do not like, it may help to give your child a choice between that picture and another one showing a new or already-liked food. For example: "Do you want to colour the picture of the chicken or the melon first?" Stay relaxed and don't expect your child to go for the disliked food straight away.

It may be fun to look up images or photographs of new foods together, so your child can see what they look like. You could talk about how the food is made or grown, or about where in the world it comes from.

# Day 18: Oral sensitivity

As we saw on Day 16, some adults and children are more sensitive to sensory stimulation than others (hyper-responsive). This can include stimulation from tastes and textures.

Children who are more sensitive to tastes and textures may try and avoid certain foods to prevent sensory overload. This is sometimes referred to as "tactile defensiveness"[1] or "oral defensiveness".

They may also be more cautious about trying new foods[2]. This is where messy play can help – it familiarises children who are more sensitive to tactile stimulation with the feeling of different textures on their hands.

Children who are more sensitive to sensory stimulation are more likely to be fussy[3]. You may have noticed that your child is more sensitive to the feeling of clothes against his skin, to sounds or smells, or to bright lights and lots of colour. Researchers have found an association between smell sensitivity and food pickiness[4] in children under 2. This is perhaps not surprising, given how important smell is for taste.

## Another perspective

Some children who were introduced to solid foods later than usual struggle to cope with foods with more texture. They may also have hypersensitivity in the mouth, and sometimes an extreme gag reflex[5].

Others may have conditions, such as autism, which often come with sensory processing issues.

Naoki Higashida is a young Japanese man with autism who, aged just 13, wrote a book ('*The Reason I Jump*') about his experiences of living with the condition[6].

Although he did not struggle with picky eating himself, Higashida explains why someone on the autistic spectrum may have difficulties with some foods. He says that a person might only be able to make sense of food, and its unique taste, texture and colour, if he already understands that the thing is an edible substance, or what we call food.

Keep trying, he tells us. It might just be that a person with autism needs just a little bit longer to get used to the food.

### Help with sorting

On Day 10, I talked about the categorisation of foods.

Foods can be divided into categories based on food group (such as fruit), based on categories that go together (such as breakfast foods) or based on our assessment of the food (nice, disgusting).

By the age of four, most children are able to categorise foods in a similar way to adults[7], including putting a particular food into more than one category. Colour and appearance are particularly important characteristics by which children categorise food; perhaps because they have less *experience* of the food the adults. This may explain young children's reluctance to eat food in sauce or mixed foods.

This might be why seeing foods increases children's acceptance of new foods[8] – it helps them to put new food into the category of 'edible and acceptable'.

Techniques that help children put unfamiliar foods into the category of edible, and into other food categories, may help them accept new foods[9]. These activities could include food naming, storytelling and the food exposure activities discussed in yesterday's chapter.

## Supertasters

On Day 12 I wrote about supertasters and their ability to detect the bitter taste of PTC and PROP.

Research also suggests that supertasters may be more sensitive to pain in the mouth[10].

Supertasters seem to feel pain and discomfort from:

- Foods such as chilli and pepper
- Very cold drinks
- Bubbling in fizzy drinks
- (Possibly) sour tastes[11]

Supertasters also experience heat in the mouth more acutely than non-tasters[12]. This may help explain some oral sensitivity; and why oral sensitivity and food pickiness seem to occur in the same toddlers.

Research has shown that sensitivity to texture and food pickiness often go hand-in-hand in 1-to-4-year-olds[13]. This is not surprising, given that a young child's instinct is to avoid anything that might be contaminating.

**Super-sweet, super-bitter, super-textured**

People who can taste PTC and PROP, or who are supertasters of PTC and PROP (this means that they have inherited the gene from both parents), also find sweet foods and drinks sweeter than the rest of us[14].

PROP supertasters experience the sweetness of saccharine more intensely than other people – *and* the bitterness that's also present in saccharine. This may explain why saccharine tastes more bitter to some people than to others.

Supertasters also experience the textures of food differently to the rest of us. They can 'feel' the fat in foods like salad dressing, dairy products and oils more than non-tasters[15]. This may explain why children who are orally sensitive prefer blander foods.

On the positive side, research has also shown that supertasters tend to be slimmer than non-tasters. They also experience the burn of alcohol and nicotine more than non-tasters, and so are less likely to drink and smoke[16].

Finally, researchers have shown that supertasters are more sensitive to pain[17] and to smells[18].

### Touch tests

Interestingly, one group of researchers showed that in 47 children with feeding problems, aged between 9 and 34 months, the children were more likely to shy away from being touched.

The researchers also found that the children's mothers were less likely to touch the child in an affectionate way[19]. Studies have shown how important touch is to infants, and how it helps children become less reactive to stress as they grow up[20].

Touch can have a surprising effect on feeding and eating.

## Adults: still disgusted!

Paul Rozin is a professor of psychology at the University of Pennsylvania, USA. Much of his recent research has been on disgust – in particular, disgust in relation to food and eating.

In a 2015 study that he was involved in, a group of 489 adults were asked to complete a questionnaire to identify whether or not they were picky eaters[21]. They were also asked about specific food preferences, such as taste, texture and colour.

Picky eaters were more likely to reject bitter or sour foods, as we would expect. They were also more likely to reject foods that had a 'slimy or slippery' texture. We would expect this, too, given our knowledge about the evolutionary reasons for food neophobia, food refusal and food pickiness that we have explored so far.

What was surprising is that Paul Rozin's research also showed that:

- Picky eaters were more likely to reject foods of certain *colours* – although there was no pattern to which colours they would reject (some people would reject one colour, some rejected other colours).

- Picky eaters were more likely to reject foods with lumps in, or foods that were combined, like a sandwich with several different fillings.
- Picky eaters were more likely not to want their foods to touch on the plate.

Does all of this sound familiar?

Around half of those who completed Paul Rozin's questionnaire were also asked to taste solutions of different strengths of sweet and bitter solutions.

### Sweet rewards

As we might expect, picky eaters were much more sensitive to the bitter-tasting solution than those who were not picky eaters. Interestingly, they were also more sensitive to the sweet-tasting solution.

We know that sweet taste is satisfying – it stimulates a part of the brain known as the reward centre, releasing a hormone called dopamine. Dopamine is known as 'the feel-good hormone'.

From the results of this research, we might conclude that picky eaters get much more of a reward from eating sweet foods than those who are not picky eaters.

## Taking action

You might be thinking, "All of this is very interesting, but how does this help my child to eat a greater range of foods?"

The answer: "Through repeated exposure!"

Even for children who are very sensitive to sensory information, repeated exposure can help. This is particularly the case in an environment where parents are able to support the child through any anxiety.

We think that the environment may actually change how taste receptors work[22]. Children who are more sensitive to touch are often pickier eaters[23], possibly because of the texture of food[24]. Exposure to the feeling of food (tactile exposure) and the look of food (visual exposure) might help too[25]. This is where 'messy play' (yesterday's exercise) comes into its own.

## Day 18: Try this at home

See for yourself if you are a supertaster, a taster or non-taster: Just see how many taste buds (fungiform papillae) you have on your tongue.

It is possible to make a reasonably accurate self-diagnosis at home by careful examination of the tongue.

- You're looking for the number of taste buds. They are the tiny knobs all over your tongue, usually a bit redder than the rest of your tongue. In an area about 6mm round (about the size of a pencil eraser):
    - An average taster has around 15-35 taste buds;
    - A supertaster has around 35-60.
- Blue food dye can make this easier – just a tiny coating using a cotton bud is enough.
- You could also try taking a high-resolution photo of your tongue and counting the taste buds in the picture.
- You can do the above for your child, your child's other parent, and any siblings. This will give you a good idea of where you are as a family.

If you're *really* keen to know, you can buy strips of paper impregnated with PTC online to test whether you are a supertaster – just search for "PTC taste sticks".

# Day 19: Boundaries and Routines

We will now switch back from biologically influenced food responses to learning and other behavioural responses.

Young children need firm boundaries and predictable routines. This applies equally to food and mealtimes[1].

Children are less likely to be fussy eaters if they have structured family meals[2]. Whatever rules apply to one child must also apply to the other children in the household (and preferably parents, too!). Research has shown that having different food rules for one child can lead to eating problems[3].

I often encounter parents who suspect their child might be on the autistic spectrum because their child demonstrates a need for routine. Occasionally this turns out to be the case, but often it is not. Put simply, young children *like* routine. They have little control over their environment and external events, and so they need predictability.

## Out of control

Young children need to know what to expect. Being consistent helps them cope and stay calm[4]. When they do not know what to expect, or what is coming next, even children who are otherwise developing well can get anxious. This anxiety often expresses itself as a meltdown or tantrum.

Young children are not in charge of the day – we decide this as parents. You only have to imagine how you might experience it yourself if somebody were to take charge of your day; if you had to go along with whatever this person wanted to do and you did not know beforehand what was going to happen, nor what to expect.

How would you feel: Uncomfortable? Worried? Out of control?

Predictable routines make young children comfortable. If the routine changes, you should let your child know what is happening and what to expect. Use terms and words she will understand. This applies to food and mealtimes, too. You may know (because you are in charge and have decided this) that when you get into town and have done one or two jobs, you will find somewhere to have a bite to eat. Let your child know what the plan is too, rather than leaving her to guess.

## Rules & regularity

When it comes to mealtime routines, young children need three regular meals and two or three regular snacks each day. These should be served at fairly regular times.

Young children need their mealtimes to be predictable, and they need to know what is expected of them:

### No pressure – but no cooking to order

They don't have to try to eat anything in particular – but there will be no alternatives (no cooking to order, nor making anything different if every food on offer is rejected).

Your child will learn this by experience when you do not prepare several alternatives in an attempt to get her to eat something – anything! More about this on Day 20.

### Sitting nicely

On the topic of sitting, how your child sits can make eating easier or harder. Make sure your child sits in a highchair that supports her feet. Adjust the chair so that her knees and elbows are at 90° angles.

### Consistency

Be consistent. Consistency really is the key to introducing healthier eating habits for children[5].

This means your rules today are the same as tomorrow. If your child knows that, if she refuses dinner, you will eventually break and give her crisps instead, then every mealtime will be a struggle.

This is not to say that this will be easy. We know that children's temperaments vary and that parents' approach to food and mealtimes is often influenced by a child's temperament[6]. It may be tempting to give in to your toddler, but chances are this will only make the next mealtime more difficult.

Stand firm but be matter-of-fact with boundaries around food. If you get anxious, angry or upset, she will respond in the same way.

Children eat poorly when emotions run high. Getting into an argument over food is counter-productive. You cannot make a young child eat and, if mealtimes become a negative experience, she will respond by eating less, not more. Try to remember that she is probably not purposefully trying to upset you, but just responding in a way that is natural for a toddler. Being stubborn is her way of becoming her own little person, distinct from mum and dad.

## Magic words

I have found that many parents have found this simple phrase to be a lifesaver:

*"You don't have to eat it."*

I'm not sure why this simple phrase is so powerful. I think it is partly because it conveys a message to the child: She is in control of whether or not to eat this food.

It also sends the message that, *because* she isn't expected to eat it, there will be no power struggle.

With this phrase goes the promise that there will be no alternatives, either; and no attention for refusing.

If a child is anxious about trying new food, she can go at her own pace – try a bit, or not, depending on how comfortable she feels experimenting at this particular meal. For parents, this phrase seems to relieve the anxiety that they *must* get their child to eat this food right now; whether for the sake of the child's nutrition and wellbeing or to remain in control of the situation.

Don't let mealtimes become a battleground. Stay calm, but firm. Your boundaries are there to protect your child. They are there to let her learn to like a healthy diet and a wide range of foods.

- You don't beg or cajole her to eat more than her appetite dictates.
- You don't plead with her to try a food.
- You don't put her under any pressure to eat.
- You don't offer bribes in an attempt to get her to eat something. (This will always backfire. She will not learn to like the food for its own sake, only in order to get the reward.)

Maintain your boundaries and stay firm and calm. Remember, she doesn't have to eat it; and nothing you do can make her eat anything anyway.

Whatever you do, don't get angry with your child. For the most part, remember that she is not trying to be obstinate nor inconsiderate towards you. She is just displaying a natural toddler behaviour, re-enforced by what she has learnt from your responses to how she eats and behaves at mealtimes.

## Day 19: Try this at home

Today's exercise is intended to get you thinking about how often you present your child with meals and snacks.

I want you to think about whether food is planned by you or offered when your child asks for it.

Over the next three days, make a note of the time each time your child eats. Note down, too, whether this was planned by you, or at the request of your child.

As usual, I've included an example to show you what I mean.

Also note whether there are any long gaps between a meal or snack, and if so, what effect, if any, this has on your child's eating at the meal or snack that follows.

| **Example Day** *Thursday* | | |
|---|---|---|
| Time | Planned or requested? | How well did *Emily* eat? |
| *07.05* | *Planned breakfast* | *Emily ate most of her Weetabix and a few pieces of fruit – quite well* |

| **Day 1** ______________ | | |
|---|---|---|
| Time | Planned or requested? | How well did ____________ eat? |
| | | |
| | | |
| | | |
| | | |
| | | |
| | | |
| | | |

| Day 2 ______________ | | |
|---|---|---|
| Time | Planned or requested? | How well did ___________ eat? |
| | | |
| | | |
| | | |
| | | |
| | | |
| | | |
| | | |

| Day 3 ______________ | | |
|---|---|---|
| Time | Planned or requested? | How well did ___________ eat? |
| | | |
| | | |
| | | |
| | | |
| | | |
| | | |
| | | |

# Day 20: Don't Offer Alternatives (and Don't Cater to Your Child)

"*What?!*" I hear some of you exclaiming. This is possibly the most controversial chapter of this book.

Many parents make a separate meal for a picky eater[1] or even change the meals they have planned for the whole family.

"How am I going to get him to eat anything at all when he refuses everything I have put out?" you may be thinking. "How will I get him to eat if I don't make what he likes?"

On Day 19 we talked about how you cannot make a young child eat food they do not want to eat – at least not consistently, and not without creating problems later on. All you can do is create the right conditions to maximise the possibility that he will eat as much as he needs.

We have also talked about how young children eat less well when they are put under pressure to eat. One of the reasons for this might be that it raises your expectations of them.

Another might be because parents' anxiety over food and eating becomes an opportunity to exert some control over you, his parents, or over his environment more generally; an environment which he otherwise has little control over.

## Emotional escalation

By offering alternatives when your young child refuses to eat from the foods already on offer, you automatically up the ante. This signals anxiety and worry on your part. He will respond by eating less well.

If he then refuses the *second* food offering – perhaps of something made to order – you will become even more emotional, because now he has refused something that you have gone to some effort to prepare specially.

The same goes if you cater to your child.

## Cooking to order

It's OK to allow a young child some say over some mealtimes: the same say as everybody else in the family. It's *not* OK if your child's wishes dictate family mealtimes.

First, this does nothing to expand his food choices, as young children will usually go for a safe and familiar option.

Second, you will be more anxious, angry and upset if he refuses the meal or foods on offer when they have been specifically requested. This heightened expectation puts more pressure on your child, who is likely to respond by eating less.

## Unhealthy options

The other reason for not offering alternatives is that these will nearly always be less healthy choices.

Children who are otherwise healthy will get the calories they need and, given the chance, will get them from tasty foods that are easy to consume.

For example:

- Children who were fussy eaters in the UK *Avon Longitudinal Study of Parents and Children* drank more fizzy drinks than children who were not fussy eaters.
- Children who were classed as "persistent" fussy eaters ate 26% more biscuits and cookies and 33% more chocolate than children in *any* of the other fussy eating groups, let alone the children who were not fussy eaters.

Just keep them out of the house or, at the very least, out of sight. This is far more effective than having these foods in plain sight and having to say "no".

## What about choice?

Young children have not yet developed the reasoning capability needed to weigh up multiple options, and the outcome and consequences of all of those options. This is why, if you ask what he wants for tea or dinner, he will tend to pick the same thing every time.

Don't get me wrong, you can offer *some* choice. This allows your child a sense of personal power and control.

It is usually best if this choice is of two desirable options. For example, you might ask:

*"Do you want Weetabix for breakfast, or toast?"*

If you ask an open question, and your child picks coco pops for the eleventh day running, you are left with two options:

1. You give him a breakfast that you know is not healthy and is doing nothing to expand his choice of food.
2. You say "no," and decide for him. This is likely to lead to a meltdown.

It would have been better to have given a limited choice of two options you were happy with from the outset.

We will discuss choice and power more on Day 25.

## Day 20: Try this at home

Today's exercise is a reflective one. You'll be thinking about what usually happens in your family when your child refuses the food on offer.

I am going to ask you to think about the 'when's and 'what's of offering alternatives on demand – and about the results.

Start by thinking about times in the last week **when** your child refused the food on offer. Can you remember these incidents?

**What** did your child end up having to eat instead? Was this a sweet or snacky food item; or a 'child-friendly' one? Was this food of lower nutritional value than the foods originally on offer?

What was **the result** of offering alternatives on demand? I suspect that your child ate something when you were concerned that he might not eat at all. You might have been relieved because you didn't have to worry that your child wasn't eating. Relieved also because the meal didn't turn into too much of a battleground.

### What about the longer-term result?

Have you tried offering the same foods (previously refused) again?

Did your child accept these? Or maybe your child has refused other meals since then, and has had the alternative at other meals or snacks since?

Without judgement, or blaming yourself, try to observe the times when your child ends up with something different from that originally planned.

I have referred to Ellyn Satter's work in previous chapters. She uses the term that parents decide the "when", "where" and "what" of meals and food; while children decide the "if" and "how much".

Using this framework, how often is your child deciding the "what"?

# Day 21: Ignoring Unwanted Behaviour

Children want our attention.

It seems strange, but they want that attention whether it is good or bad.

Generally, adults like to keep out of the way of negative attention, like making other people feel bad and being told off. This is a social norm: behaviour that we learn as we grow up.

Think about how you respond to criticism at work, and the difficulties you may have in saying, "No".

## Attention means survival

Young children are still learning about social responses. Many, if not most, of these responses developed in humans to enable us to live effectively in a group. Social niceties maximise our potential for survival.

In contrast, children would have needed to keep the constant attention of their caregivers in order to maximise *their* potential for survival. This would have been particularly relevant when resources were scarce, and there were many young mouths to feed and youngsters to take care of.

Constantly being within the attention span of caregivers (parents and other family members) means that children are more likely to survive. You're more likely to notice if a lion approaches with the intention of having your little one for dinner!

Demanding attention and protection are survival mechanisms. Learning the finer human skills of cooperation, negotiation and sharing come later.

But what does this have to do with refusing food?

Young children will try and keep your constant attention. This includes at the dinner table, and particularly if a child is 'competing' with siblings or other children. Food refusal is often a very effective way of getting your attention, precisely because we are designed to worry so much about it.

Food refusal and other childish eating behaviours (like pushing food around, chewing and chewing and chewing, and spitting out) get us focused on the child demonstrating them.

### Poker face practice

So, as hard as it is, dust off that Oscar and try to ignore these behaviours. Don't ignore the child, just the behaviour. So, ignore the pushing around the plate and screwed up face. Keep chatting, chat about the day, school, playgroup, what Granny said, what you're going to do later, their new friend or toy. You get the picture. Ignore the behaviour, and it's just not fun anymore. And more importantly, it doesn't get any attention.

If you offer and prepare alternatives, beg, cajole, coax or bribe your child to eat or, worse still, feed her beyond the age when help with eating is needed, you are giving attention to food refusal. It also gives your child control over you, at least at mealtimes. All of these actions on your part will lead to more battles at the dinner table.

## What about begging for food?

Ignore this, too.

This is especially hard because the very reason you are reading this book and following this programme is that you *want* your child to eat. Not giving your child food when she asks for it seems counter-intuitive.

You should, by now, have a routine of three meals and two or three snacks each day, at fairly regular intervals (see Day 19).

The reason you should ignore any begging for food is that it doesn't get your child into the habit of eating as much as she needs at regular, planned times.

She is likely to fill up if food is offered between these times; so, she eats less well at the next snack or meal… and you are now in a vicious cycle.

Don't get me wrong: I don't recommend that children are made to go hungry in an attempt to improve their appetites. Children also eat less well when they are over-hungry. Just stick to the three meals and two or three snacks pattern.

### Unscheduled and unhealthy

If your child is asking for food between your planned times, she is probably angling for less healthy options.

Offering food between scheduled meals and snacks also gives your child control over the whole feeding and eating process. Remember the "the division of responsibility" maxim from Day 15 (coined by Ellyn Satter): parents decide "what, when and where" food is eaten, and children decide "if" and "how much" they will eat.

What should you do if she begs for food between planned meal and snack times? Explain once why she cannot have the food in question and then ignore the begging.

Do not get into a long-winded debate back and forth about why you're refusing. Explain once ("It's not snack time yet.") and move on. Start an activity or find another distraction.

## Behaviours to ignore

What about some of these odd-but-irritating toddler behaviours at the dinner table?

If a behaviour is just one of those quirks of children, and not offensive, then ignore it. Paying attention may just make your child want to do it more, to get a reaction.

That's an important distinction: Whether your child is trying to get a reaction from you. If you suspect she is using a mealtime behaviour to get a reaction, you must ignore it.

If your older child behaves in a way that is rude to others, then say no – only once – and then ignore her. If she doesn't stop the behaviour after a few seconds, then ask her to leave the table. She is probably not that hungry and was not going to eat very well at this meal anyway. Don't allow her to return to the table. Next time, she will know that bad behaviour means being sent away from the table.

## What to accept (but still ignore!)

Ignore behaviour that you don't want to see more of. But do keep in mind that some behaviours, while not acceptable for older children and adults, are part of the normal development of younger children as they learn to eat.

Often, they are just working out how to manage a new food. This includes behaviours such as pushing food around the plate, mashing it up, and otherwise playing with it. Think of it as practice.

*Mouthing*

Another example of a child's behaviour to ignore is "mouthing". Mouthing is when a young child puts food in her mouth and takes it out again. Sometimes a child will even chew the food and take it out, which may be accompanied by a grimace.

Toddlers may "mouth" a new food many times while they get used to the flavour and the texture.

Young children learn to like new tastes, flavours and textures by trying them out. I have already mentioned that children eat better when they are not put under pressure to eat. This includes not being put under pressure to actually *swallow* the food. It is perfectly OK for your child to experiment by putting unfamiliar food in her mouth and taking it back out again.

Tasting the food makes it more familiar. With every attempt at tasting new food, often over several meals or snacks, the food becomes more familiar. When it is more familiar, there is a bigger chance that your child will learn to like it.

By putting food in and taking it out, I mean politely removing the food and putting it back on her plate. I don't mean spitting out, heaving up nor making exaggerated yuk sounds, whining, crying or saying how disgusting it is. Teach your child to politely take food out and put it back on the plate if she doesn't fancy swallowing it today.

This process was covered in more detail in our experiment with Tiny Tastes on Day 14.

Of course, mouthing food is really only acceptable for younger children. Once your child has reached 3 or 4 years old, she should have had the chance to try a range of tastes and textures. She should by now be including most of these new foods in her diet.

But there are still some unfamiliar foods to go. Even adults have new food experiences from time to time. Or maybe your child has had a bit of rocky start with trying new foods, and that's why you're reading this book. She should still remove food politely.

If she is old enough to understand, then she can be taught to remove uneaten food into a napkin or paper towel. If mastered with enough subtlety, this is something she can even do as an adult (although, we would hope, not too often!).

*Grimacing*

Young children are just learning how to control their facial expressions in a socially acceptable way (hey, I know adults unable to control their grimacing at my cooking!).

Just don't focus on it; or else she may learn that gurning is an excellent way to get your full attention at a mealtime (rather than, say, practising good eating behaviour).

### What not to accept

Behaviours that are not acceptable even for younger children include throwing food, forcefully spitting food or pretending to vomit for effect.

## Vomiting and gagging...

Speaking of vomiting for effect, I'd like to make a note.

I discussed this in a post on my Facebook page. The post created some controversy, as I had included advice to ignore retching and vomiting.

I am not suggesting that a parent ignores a vomiting child if that child may be ill. But if, in your heart of hearts, you think that this is part of food refusal? Then ignore it.

### ...for effect

Parents often see the advent of this vomiting when they start ignoring food refusal.

The refusal often escalates a bit first; the child might try pushing food off the plate, spitting it out, making more fuss about how disgusting the food is, etc.

Vomiting (or, rather, retching and spitting) comes when all else has failed. You may have even noticed your little one looking out of the corner of their eye to see whether you are noticing and/or responding.

I met a young family as I was writing this book; dad had already worked out that the retching, regurgitating and spitting usually resulted in mum making something different for their little boy. The end result was that, to avoid this mealtime ritual, the little lad ended up getting chicken nuggets for dinner every day. At first, this wasn't a huge problem. But as time went on, and he wasn't experiencing new foods at mealtimes, his parents had to start asking other family members to cook chicken nuggets (and a particular brand, at that) for him at family gatherings. By the time I met the family, he was six and had started school.

Naturally, vomiting makes parents anxious. We care for our children and don't want to see them ill. But do not allow such pretend vomiting to scupper your resolve of not paying attention to food refusal and not offering replacements.

If a child is unwell, then tucking them in bed is probably best. If you suspect *fake* vomiting (as opposed to *real* vomiting), then you must use the same strategies with this behaviour as you would with other behaviours that are unacceptable. Tell her to stop and ignore the behaviour (but bring your child back into the conversation and attention once she has stopped). If this fails, then you may need to warn her that this is not allowed at the dinner table; and, if she is unable to stop, then she will have to leave the dinner table.

### ...due to illness

Ill or not, vomiting is never good; mainly because of the potential for food aversions. Humans are very good at making the association between food consumed and any gastrointestinal ill effects, like vomiting. This can then lead to food aversions.

Anybody who has had food poisoning, or been sick during pregnancy, will recognise this. If a food (or drink) makes us gastrointestinally unwell, then the taste, smell, and even the thought of that food can start to turn our stomachs – sometimes forever (although repeated exposure does work wonders here too, even for adults).

Vomiting is closely related to disgust. The sensation of purging and the drive to vomit is a very strong human reaction that protects us against poisoning. If a type of food has previously made us ill, then our associative memory will trigger the urge to vomit if we eat, and sometimes even smell, that food again.

My best friend was unable to drink or even stomach the smell of red bush tea for a long time after her second child was born. I was carsick on peanuts as a kid and couldn't bear the smell of them for years.

The technique to overcome these urges is repeated exposure. Start with the sight of the food, then the smell. Smell, smell, smell, smell… and then, one day, a tiny taste.

I eat peanut butter with gusto now, although I still can't bear the taste of peanuts in other foods.

### ...due to difficulty eating

Vomiting and gagging can also be a child's way of trying not to eat when eating is too hard due to, for example, swallowing difficulties or previous bad experiences with food.

If you suspect your child has any difficulties with swallowing, then you must take her to the GP or Family Doctor. Your child's GP or Family Doctor may be able to rule out any underlying medical difficulties and refer her, if necessary, to a paediatrician; speech and language therapist/pathologist; physiotherapist/physical therapist; and/or an occupational therapist.

If your child has been ill or gagged on a type of food in the past, then she might automatically gag and retch, even vomit, when presented with this food again.

This is a natural human reaction to food that has previously made us ill. Past illness is the basis of many food aversions. In this case, there is little that you can do, other than to keep offering the offending food – without pressure or expectation. One day, your child might take a tiny bite or lick.

Familiarity with the offending food may have the same effect as familiarity with new foods. If the food doesn't make her ill again, then she may well be brave and try some. Or she may not. You might have to accept that some foods are just going to be too difficult.

Or you might try the food chaining method that I will describe on Day 27, or refer back to repeated food exposure on Days 13 and 14.

## Gagging

Gagging can be irritating for parents, as well as a source of worry. Your young child is still learning to eat – and part of this learning includes experimenting.

I always reframe this as "practice" with parents, which seems to work. A 30-year-old adult will probably have eaten…

30 years x 5 meals or snacks per day x 365 days per year =

…nearly 55,000 meals or snacks in our lifetime. This is 55,000 eating practices. If it takes 10,000 practices of something to become a master then, by the time we are 30, we are a master five times over. This is why it is so easy for us to eat or drink and do other things at the same time. We call this "eating mindlessly".

ⓘ

*Choking is not the same as gagging!*

Young children are at risk of choking as they learn to eat. They shouldn't be left unsupervised with food or drink. See below.

Young children have to keep practising. Part of this practice includes working out how much to put in their mouths to be able to move it around, to chew it and to swallow it without gagging or choking.

Getting it wrong from time to time, and gagging, as a result, is part of the process.

Gagging, then, is usually another behaviour to ignore. If you pay too much attention to it, your toddler may learn that it is another excellent way of getting your attention.

### Making it easy

It helps young children to learn to eat and feel good about their newly developing skills if parents provide food of a texture that they can manage and practise with, and the right utensils to help.

This might mean offering softer foods for a while, chopping food up, providing toddler-friendly utensils to use, and not worrying if she resorts to using her hands when things get too hard.

### Staying safe

There are a few foods to avoid offering young children because they can be a risk for choking. This includes foods that are roundish, smooth and about the size of a child's airway, where they can get stuck and cause choking. For children under 5, avoid:

- Whole nuts
- Round slices of raw carrot
- Hard sweets/candy, gumdrops, jellybeans, and mini chocolate eggs
- Seeds (for example, sunflower or watermelon)
- Popcorn
- Chunks of peanut butter
- Raisins
- Chunks of meat or cheese
- Chewing gum

You can adapt some foods that may cause a choking hazard. For example, cut hot dogs lengthwise, quarter grapes and cherry tomatoes, peel and grate raw apples and carrots, and chop nuts finely.

And *always* pay attention while your child eats.

## Table manners

Children take a while to learn how to use cutlery, so they may eat with their fingers.

Thcy need to get lots of practice to learn how to use cutlery effectively. They also need lots of opportunities to watch adults use knives and forks. This is another reason to eat with your child as much as possible.

### Cutlery

Don't worry too much about using cutlery correctly – at least not to start with. Your child will soon learn by watching the adults and any older siblings.

When a child is a picky eater, one of the key sensations she must get used to is the feeling of food. This helps her to become familiar with new food and learn that it poses no threat. By feeling the texture of unfamiliar food in her hands, she may anticipate what this new food will feel like when eaten.

So, to start with, don't insist on cutlery. Just carry on using your own cutlery and, once your child has become familiar and comfortable with the new food, she will usually follow your lead and try and copy you. Give her lots of praise for doing so.

Your child will take great pride in being able to eat like the adults, so don't tell her off if she doesn't get it right to start with. Remember to give lots of praise whenever she does get it right (or almost right).

Expect spills and mess!

## Drinking

I also recommend that children drink from an open cup as soon as they are able to learn to do this. It is much better for their teeth. It also helps them learn the very complex skills needed to get food and drink in the right place and down the right way.

## Sitting at the table

The one thing I do insist on is that young children should sit, and stay seated, at the adult table.

There are occasional exceptions to this: Picnics, parties, eating out, or dining with friends where the children have their own little table, for example. Otherwise, children should sit with adults. This allows young children to watch what and how adults eat – your child will learn lots from this.

Young children should stay at the table as long as they are eating.

Once your child is finished, let her get down. If she starts messing around, let her down. Don't make a child stay at the table for a long time in the hope that she will eat more – she won't. Children have a short attention span, and forcing their presence just makes mealtimes unpleasant.

Just 20 to 30 minutes is enough; maybe even less for a small snack.

When I was running a healthy family food programme in Wales, we asked parents to complete questionnaires about the programme, to gauge how helpful it had been for them. To our initial surprise, the part of the programme that parents found consistently most useful was our advice to limit mealtimes to 20 to 30 minutes.

Finally, you shouldn't allow your child to run around and come back to the table. When eating is over, it is over. She can now wait until the next meal or planned snack.

## Day 21: Try this at home

I'm now going to ask you to first list five foods that your child will eat, followed by five foods that your child won't eat.

You're then going to try and think of how many times you have force-fed, begged, bribed or (otherwise) coerced your child to eat each of the ten foods now on your list.

Think carefully!

As usual, I have filled in a couple of examples.

**Note:** This exercise can bring up some negative feelings for parents who have acted out of frustration or fear for their child's nutrition. Please remember that the point of this programme is not to feel bad about your past actions but to bring positivity to future ones. When you have finished the table, you may like to write down any emotions that have surfaced as a result of the exercise.

| Food | Likes/ dislikes? | Force-fed | Begged | Bribed | Other coercion |
|---|---|---|---|---|---|
| *Broccoli* | *Hates* | *Never!* | *I have begged him to eat it for Mummy.* | *I often say he can only have pudding if he eats his broccoli* | *I have said that he should eat it otherwise he'll get sick like grandad* |
| *Yoghurt* | *Loves it* | *Never* | *Don't need to* | *Don't need to* | *Don't need to* |
| | | | | | |
| | | | | | |
| | | | | | |
| | | | | | |
| | | | | | |

# Day 22: Giving Effective Praise

Young children need to feel successful at mealtimes.

Some child-rearing experts disagree with giving children praise. They argue that praise can be manipulative, getting a child to do what a parent wants, and doesn't allow a child to want to do the activity for their own sake[1].

Giving a child praise does, however, let him know that he has done well, or pleased you.

## Unconditional praise

Praise has to be unconditional. What do I mean by this? Compare the two examples below:

*"Wow, look at you, eating the same as Mummy and Daddy!"*

Or…

*"Wow, look at you, eating the same as Mummy and Daddy! Now, can you eat the rest?"*

In the first example, the child is left feeling good about himself – he has achieved something.

In the second, the child has been praised… sort of. He is left feeling that he hasn't done *quite* well enough – that a little more was expected. And, if one or two bites is all he can manage today, then he is probably left thinking that he hasn't done very well at all.

What do you think might happen when he encounters the new food again?

We very often give praise, and other positive acknowledgements, to our children and other people conditionally. By conditionally, I mean including a caveat (whether explicit or implied). "But..."

For example:

- To your spouse or partner: "That wall looks great now you have painted it, but we need to get the doors done too."
- To a member of staff: "Thank you so much for getting the report done, that was really helpful; but could you also send it to the board?"
- To a young child: "Well done for getting your shoes on all by yourself, but you need to get the straps tighter next time."

At the dinner table, we might say to the same child: "Well done for trying a few peas. Now, can you eat them all up?"

## Things left undone

This habit doesn't mean we're bad people – it's just how we tend to respond, as humans. It might have something to do with what psychologists call "negativity bias". We tend to look for the "But…".

I often come across this when working with adults. I might ask: "How did you get on with x?"

"Not very well," is often the response.

When we explore this a little further, it turns out they *have* made loads of changes. But our instinct is to focus on what still needs to be done; all the things that we should have done but haven't.

## Feeling deflated

Can you remember a time you've received conditional praise? I can think of a few times it's happened to me, both at work and at home.

How does it make you feel? A bit deflated?

I certainly felt something along the lines of, "Well, if I'm only going to get negativity, I won't bother next time."

This might be how it feels to a toddler who has made a huge effort to overcome his instinctive fear of this unfamiliar food – a food that tastes strange and feels odd – and is looking to a parent or caregiver for positive affirmation. Deflating.

Which will probably make him less likely to try it again next time.

**Over-the-top is perfect**

Give lots and lots of unconditional praise for any trying and other mealtime behaviours you want more of. All the time. Keep it up.

*"Well done, you have sat so well through lunch."*

*"Well done - you tried the peas!"*

*"Look at you, you've tried the fishcake!"*

You see what I mean. Just keep it coming.

A nursery nurse I used to work with said: "Over-the-top, sickly praise". This helps make trying a new, scary food fun for a child.

Just make sure you are praising *trying*; not praising your child for each and every mouthful, in an attempt to get your child to finish everything *you* want him to eat.

What about if your little one displays behaviour you want (and you responded, "Well done you!") and then immediately follows it with behaviour you don't want?

Look away. Ignore it. Say something to another child or person at the table. Help yourself to a little more. Reach for the salt or pepper.

Watch out of the corner of your eye, and as soon as you see a behaviour you *do* want, get straight back in there.

*"Well done, look at you, using your fork like a grown-up."*

Unconditional praise is so effective, it can be used with older children and even adults (although, perhaps, you can tone down the over-the-top, sickly praise!).

## Day 22: Try this at home

For the next few days, keep a note in a diary or on your phone every time you hear the explicit or implied "But…" of conditional praise.

This might be at home, at work, from friends or family members. It doesn't have to be in the context of food or eating – just people going about their everyday lives.

You might even catch yourself using it, either with other people or to yourself. Note this down as well!

# Day 23: Treats and Bribes (Managing Behaviour with Food)

On Day 11, we discussed three effective strategies for increasing a child's liking of a new sort of food.

Today is all about methods you *shouldn't* use to increase your child's liking of new food – in particular, bribing and rewarding.

A common strategy for parents desperate to get their child to eat is to offer a more desirable food to their toddler as a reward for eating less desirable food.

For example, "You can have pudding [dessert, for you State-siders] if you eat your vegetables."

I recommend that you do *not* use this strategy, as it reinforces to a child the message that one food (the pudding) is more desirable than the other food (the vegetables), which the child must be bribed to eat.

## Rewards can backfire

Research has shown that children who are rewarded for eating tend to eat less well[1].

A systematic review* in 2017 of factors related to picky eating in young children found a clear relationship between offering rewards for eating and fussy eating habits[2].

We know that young children learn to prefer foods that are used as rewards, or that are accompanied by attention from adults.

Behaviours learned as children continue in adults. One study, of 684 university students in Turkey, showed that those whose parents used food as a reward were much more likely than other students to use food as a reward for themselves once they were adults[3].

---

* A systematic review looks at all the research papers published on a topic, and usually goes to great lengths to make sure that none are missed out.

## Desirability decreasing

When we use food as a reward, researchers have found that children tend to want more of the reward food[4]. Not surprising really!

Using one food as a reward for eating another food seems to reduce the liking of the food you are trying to get a child to like, and increases the desirability of the food used as the reward[5].

## Intrinsic vs extrinsic motivation

This might be because, by offering a reward, we undermine a child's natural desires to learn, to try new things for trying's sake, and to feel proud of themselves for having achieved.

Researchers call this 'intrinsic motivation'.

Rewards are called 'extrinsic motivation' or 'extrinsic rewards'. We think that giving extrinsic rewards reduces intrinsic motivation. When we take the reward away, a child doesn't want to do the behaviour without rewards any more, even if she was quite happy to do it before[6].

If we try to encourage, coax, bribe or cajole a young child into eating a less desirable food (like vegetables) by rewarding that behaviour with a more desirable food (like chocolate), then the result will be *an increased liking for the treat food and a decreased liking for the less desirable food* (e.g. vegetables)[7].

This has been confirmed even when researchers ask groups of children to eat food they already liked.

Don't do it. Do not offer a treat food contingent on eating another part of the meal. It will only increase liking for the treat food and reduce liking of the (usually) healthier food[8].

A child may eat her broccoli at this meal, on the promise of pudding, but she will not do so at the next meal. Researchers call this the 'overjustification effect': The intrinsic desire to eat is reduced when that food becomes a way of getting a reward[9].

The Battle of the Broccoli has only just started.

## Alternative ideas

### Rewarding with words

Rewards in the form of attention and praise might seem to have a different effect.

This could be because praise makes the mealtime atmosphere more positive, and children are highly attuned to the mood at mealtimes[10]. They eat better with a positive mealtime atmosphere.

### Consistent rewards

Many modern recommendations suggest that we offer young children a pudding/dessert after each meal. The theory goes that, by offering pudding, we take the pressure off children needing to meet their nutritional needs from the main meal.

I agree with this principle – if the dessert is fruit-based or made from flour or a milk product (I am thinking fruit and custard, crumble or fruit compote with yoghurt). I disagree when dessert is a very sweet, shop-bought pudding with little in the way of nutrition.

I also don't think it's necessary to regularly offer dessert if that is not something that you do as a family. Having said that, you might add yoghurt or a bit of fruit after a meal, or a biscuit with a snack.

Where I do agree with this philosophy is that, when a dessert is offered, it should not be contingent on finishing a meal; or even part of the meal (like the vegetables). If you are having dessert, then have it regardless.

### Variety

A range of foods from a normal menu should be enough to provide some variety. Young children will likely eat a few bites of the different things on offer to meet their nutritional needs.

An example is my now infamous chilli con carne, which contains beans and tomato sauce. This will usually be served with rice, soured cream, grated cheese, perhaps some guacamole, a few nachos, and bits of salad. This meal should provide enough choice of different foods to make a good contribution to a young child's nutritional needs if she picks a few bits of most things, even if a few are left.

## Day 23: Try this at home

Over the next few days, notice if and when you are bribing or rewarding your child to eat, and if you beg, cajole or coax your child to eat.

To extend this from Day 21's exercise, reflect on the circumstances and your own feelings at the time, and whether these had any influence on your reaction.

It might then be helpful to think about how you might respond or set things up in similar circumstances in the future.

I have filled in an example.

| When and what? | Beg, cajole, coax, bribe or reward? |
| --- | --- |
| *Sunday evening roast dinner, Harry was playing up from the start, pushing food around, saying he didn't like this and the other.* | *At first, I begged him to eat just a bit of everything on his plate. When he still messed about, I said he could only have pudding (crumble) if he ate two mouthfuls of everything.* |
| | |
| | |
| | |

| Circumstances and my feelings | What would I do differently next time? |
|---|---|
| I had gone to a lot of effort to cook a roast dinner and get everything ready on time, while also getting everybody ready for the week ahead. I wanted us to have a relaxed meal before the week starts | We had had a long day, I was tired, and the kids were tired. It probably wasn't the best idea to do a roast. Next time I'll go for something easier for me, and then it doesn't matter so much if they fuss.<br>I also won't beg him, it just made him more determined not to eat |
| | |
| | |
| | |

# Day 24: Role Modelling

Today we reach the section of the programme where you, as parents, have the biggest part to play: Role modelling.

Young children are hugely influenced by observing what those around them eat[1] – it is the *most* important factor influencing dietary intake in younger children[2].

Children learn by copying their parents[3]. The younger the child, the more important the adult role models, especially trusted adults like parents (as opposed to visitors)[4]. Chances are, if you don't eat it, your child won't.

Compare, for example:

*"Look at you, eating all your tomato!"* said with a happy expression and positive voice.
(Positive response from the parent)

*"No, daddy doesn't like tomatoes either,"* screwing up his face in disgust.
(Negative response from the parent)

Young children copy you and learn from you. This includes your reactions and responses to *their* new experiences.

This helps to explain why role modelling is so important for young children to learn to like new foods and continue to enjoy old favourites.

## Imitation for survival

Observe-and-copy is a good survival instinct: "If those around me, who I trust to look after me, are eating the food, it must be safe and enjoyable. If they won't eat it, it's probably bad."

Research has shown, for example, that young children are more likely to eat fruits and vegetables if their parents do[5]. Think back again to pre-historic times – not all fruit and veg a child could come across *would* be safe.

Role modelling is also important because, as you will have noted in your own life, what we *expect* of an experience largely shapes how we will *perceive* that experience[6].

How does that work in this context? By watching parents, other adults, and children, a young child might shape how they experience new food. By judging the facial expression, response and attitude towards a new food, a child is learning his social cues. If these cues say: "Stop! This is potentially dangerous" there is no way the child is going to risk eating it.

### Changing alliances

The importance of role modelling was cleverly demonstrated in an experiment conducted by the psychologist Sibylle K. Escalona in the 1940s[7]. She worked in a prison for women.

The inmates were allowed to keep their children with them if they were under 3 years old. The children lived in the prison nursery, cared for by prison staff and visited by their mothers.

Escalona noted that some children developed either a dislike or preference for the tomato or orange juices that were served in the nursery. The two juice flavours were served on alternate days.

After some time, the children's preference would change – and then, often, change back. Escalona pinpointed that their preference was directly related to the stated favourite of whichever member of staff was assigned to look after a particular child. When the main carer changed, the child's juice preferences changed to match that of their main carer.

## Positive role modelling

Children are more likely to accept a new food if it is paired with positive words and emotional expressions[8].

Parents should be smiling, trying the food and responding to the food in a positive way. "Nam nam, this carrot tastes so sweet."

**Smile for success**

Yes, facial expressions matter, too!

For example, researchers in France wanted to see whether facial expression made adults and children want to eat a kind of food more or less when they were shown photographs of different foods.

Children, 5 and 8 years of age, and adults were given photographs of foods that they liked and foods that they didn't like.

They were shown photographs depicting:

- The food alone, or;
- The food and an adult, who is shown about to eat a piece of bread (the bread was *not* the food focused on in the photo).
    - The adult's expression was pleasant in some photos and disgusted in others.

The study showed that everyone in the study wanted to eat the food they didn't like more if the adult had a pleasant expression. *The effect was most pronounced in the 5-year-olds.*

When the photographed adult pretended to be disgusted by the bread, even if sat next to food the participants already liked, all participants wanted to eat that food less. *This was especially so for the children* – even when the food was one they already liked[9].

This shows that children are far more influenced by the facial expressions and the reaction of other people eating at the same time than adults are. Even if the other people are eating different food!

In the programme that I ran in Wales, which encouraged children aged 2-4 and 4-7 to try new foods, we actively coached parents to respond positively to new foods.

Most parents were unaware of how their own reaction to food influenced their children. Most were also unaware that they were even reacting in the ways that they were!

## Eating with peers

Another powerful influencer of children's food preferences, even in young children, is that of their peers.

I have observed this phenomenon many times, in various groups that I have run. A young child is just about to try something for the first time… only to see the tot sat opposite spit the same thing out and screw his face up. There is no way a young child observing this will have a go now!

We see this process at work in food marketing. The target demographic's peers, or peer models and role models, eat and enjoy the advertised food or drink.

When targeted at children, this marketing influences our own child to want the advertised food. The particularly strong influence of food marketing on children is why there are (some, at least) rules about marketing unhealthy foods to children.

### I will not eat blue eggs and ham...

A clever study by Janette Greenhalgh and her colleagues in the School of Psychology at Bangor University in Wales[10] demonstrates how important peer role modelling can be for children.

The researchers recruited children aged between 3 and 7. They wanted to compare how much new, *blue* food children would eat when it was modelled by older children, in comparison to just being shown the blue food.

For the first part of the study, the children were split into groups:

1. In one group, the older children ate and enjoyed the novel blue food and said positive things about the food (things they had been trained, by the researchers, to say).

2. In the second group, the older children did not eat the food but instead said negative things about the food (they, too, had been trained to say these things).

The researchers also wanted to see whether peer role modelling would have a follow on-effect on how much of other blue foods the children would eat in the future. So, for the second part of the study, the researchers made up some blue-coloured cereal bars.

*Results*

The researchers found that the children ate more of the first blue food when it was positively role modelled by older children – and virtually none when their peers were negative about the food.

This effect spilt into the second blue food: children who had heard bad things about the first blue food were not very likely to want to try another blue food! If their peers had been positive and eaten the first blue food, the children were quite likely to try another blue food when they were on their own.

## Details matter

It seems that younger children (up to 3 years old) are more likely to be influenced by parents, whereas older children are more likely to be influenced by their peers (other children)[11].

Despite this, children of *all* ages will have food choices influenced by those around them – including their parents – and it is not enough to simply be at the table. Peers and role models have to actually eat *the same thing* as a child to increase the child's willingness to try new food (or at least, it has to look like the same thing)[12]. And the more people that eat the new foods, the more likely a child is to try them[13].

It seems that the effects of seeing others eat go beyond the original meal, too – if a child sees other people eat the same food as him, then he is more likely to try it again at a later meal[14].

If influenced by a peer to try a portion of new food on a few occasions, the toddler will usually start to like this food themselves, merely through exposure, which we talked about on Day 13.

What's more, the effects of seeing our parents eating certain foods last into adulthood – we are more likely to like a food item now, *even if we disliked the same food as a child*, if we saw our parents eat that food[15].

## Modern challenges

We have no precedent for today's eating patterns. Children are designed, through millions of years of evolution, to observe and learn from those around them. This learning is based on humans' tendency to eat together.

Today's lifestyles are very different, with different demands.

We eat at different times, in a rush, and more often on our own than ever before (or even while on the move). Is it any wonder we experience problems with our children's eating?

This book aims to bring calm and enjoyment to family meals, for parents to experience mealtimes as a source of pleasure and a time for the family to come together.

**I cannot stress strongly enough the importance of children seeing adults and other children eating.**

This means eating together at mealtimes; family meals; extended family gatherings; and children eating with their peers, at school and with friends.

We can summarise Day 24 by saying that young children learn to like the foods that the adults and other children around them also like.

## Day 24: Try this at home

There are two exercises to try at home today.

The first is a reflective exercise that asks you to think back. The second is a more practical exercise that gets you "doing".

### Exercise 1: What has my toddler seen?

1. First, think of six foods that you *wish* your toddler would eat, but that they refuse.
2. Next, think about how often your toddler sees you eat each of those same foods.
3. Finally, think about who else your toddler has seen eat the foods, and how often.

As usual, I have filled in an example. (As with all of the exercises in this book, you can either use the table provided or, if you prefer, a workbook, piece of paper or any other way of recording your answers.)

| Food type | How often has my child seen me eat this food |
|---|---|
| Carrots | Only if it's on our Sunday dinner. |
| | |
| | |
| | |
| | |
| | |
| | |

| Who else have they seen eat this food? How often? | Notes |
|---|---|
| *Emily usually eats her dinner with her older brother.* | *I tried to give Emily carrots on Friday when she was eating with her older brother.* |
| | |
| | |
| | |
| | |
| | |
| | |

## Exercise 2: How does my toddler respond?

In this exercise, we will practice some touchy-feely mindfulness.

I am going to ask you to try five different foods with your child, preferably on different occasions. You could even ask other people who are involved in providing childcare to join in. I've filled in an example, to show you what I mean.

The aim is to notice whether or not there is a pattern between your (and other adults') responses to food, and the responses of your child.

| | *e.g.* |
|---|---|
| Day & Meal | *Monday snack* |
| Food | *Banana* |
| My response to the food | *I don't like banana ... I thought I was going to be sick* |
| [Other participant/s'] response to the food | *Rob (Dad): he loves banana so had no problems eating it with Emily!* |
| Child's response to the food | *She spat it out with me, but licked a bit with her dad* |
| • *What does this tell me?*<br>• *What can I learn from this?*<br>• *How might I respond differently to this food in the future?*<br>• *What needs communicating with others? How?* | *Emily is never going to eat banana with me. I can't stand it!*<br>*It's probably best if she eats it with other people.* |

| 1 | 2 | 3 | 4 | 5 |
|---|---|---|---|---|
| | | | | |
| | | | | |
| | | | | |
| | | | | |
| | | | | |
| | | | | |

# Day 25: Giving Your Child Some Control

Young children and toddlers need structure and limits. But they also want and need some choice[1].

Structure and limits help children to feel safe. By testing limits, a young child is making sure that she is noticed. When you set boundaries, and keep to them, she feels reassured that you are there and watching over her.

As young children start to develop their own sense of identity, they want some autonomy. This need for control extends into food choices. They begin to want foods that their parents don't have and to desire their own foods that they don't have to share.

Irene Chatoor, a Professor of Psychiatry and Pediatrics at the George Washington University School of Medicine, in the US, was the first researcher to suggest that feeding problems in young children were often a child's attempt to achieve autonomy from their parents[2]. Much of her research looks at food refusal that is severe enough to make a child stop growing, but some of her findings are relevant here – in particular, how mealtime battles can continue and even get worse.

Not eating is a sure-fire way of getting your parent's attention. When a child figures this out, mealtimes can quickly become a battleground.

Don't worry – there are ways of giving your child some autonomy while also making sure that she eats well.

## Reconciling structure, limits and choice

There are two elements to this chapter: Structure and limits set by the parents, and some control ceded to the child.

They are not mutually exclusive. It is possible to provide both at the dinner table.

You provide structure and limits for mealtime behaviour and routines by establishing your expectations as a family and as a parent.

- Structure includes regular, planned meals and snacks, and eating at the table without distractions. We have already discussed these essentials (Day 19).
- Limits are built by establishing, and sticking to, your rules around mealtimes and food. e.g.:
    - Not allowing snacking in between planned meals and snacks (except very occasionally)
    - Not allowing your child to run around while eating
    - Not offering alternatives when meals or snacks are refused

Today, I want to focus on giving your child some control, *within* limits, at mealtimes.

Most mealtime battles stem from our wish to get our child to eat a certain amount, a certain thing, and, whatever it is, *quickly* – so that we can get on with all the other chores we have to do in a busy family.

But trying to hurry your child at the dinner table usually backfires in the long run. You end up spending even more time preparing food that she will eat; else she gives you the run-around, and you end up making and cooking several different things at mealtimes.

A toddler starts to demonstrate autonomy by separating herself from her parents. This can be achieved, in part, by exerting her will around food – rejecting what is offered.

In this way, a toddler will try to demonstrate her autonomy, and also control her parents.

Ellyn Satter argues that a parent must allow a toddler to develop autonomy – not by allowing her to control the parent, nor indeed by parents trying to control the toddler; but by allowing toddlers to explore and develop their eating habits and food preferences with "structure and limits"[3].

By this, Satter means that parents decide what, when and where a toddler eats, and the toddler decides how much, and even whether, to eat*.

## Making it work

You, as the parent, must establish the family rules and habits regarding what is offered at a snack or mealtime, where and when this is offered.

- You will decide what time lunch is and what time tea or dinner is.
- You will decide where the family will eat. This will usually mean at a table, free from distractions. This allows your young child to tune in to her appetite and to enjoy the food with her full attention.
- If you have decided that meals (and snacks) will not be taken in front of the TV, then they shall not be taken in front of the TV. Do not fall into the trap of putting the TV on, or allowing a tablet device at the meal table, because this is the only way she will eat[4].
- Set, and stick to, rules regarding mealtimes. This also means sticking to the rules about the timing of meals and snacks. If lunch is at 12 noon, and an afternoon snack at 3 pm, do not allow snacking between those times – no matter how much your child pleads and begs.
- You decide what is to be served. Some choice can be allowed as toddlers develop – for example, "toast or Weetabix?" – but do not allow your child to determine what's on the table, either explicitly or otherwise.
    - Do not be tempted to serve only chicken nuggets and microwave chips for tea because 'at least she will eat something'. Parents must decide what is an acceptable diet and offer the diet they believe is best for their child.

Such structure allows your child to choose and exert her autonomy, within the boundaries that you have set. She will try to push those boundaries but sticking to them makes your child feel safe.

---

* You can now see how widely applicable this one piece of wisdom has been throughout our programme!

## How much choice is too much?

Parenting manuals often use the example of choosing clothes to demonstrate how you can give a child some control.

Young children struggle to make a choice when faced with multiple options ("Which outfit would you like to wear today?") which can sometimes lead to a meltdown.

Similarly, if they are allowed free rein and choose an entirely inappropriate outfit (such as a swimsuit in the middle of winter), we then have to deny them the choice we gave them. This is also likely to lead to a tantrum.

Instead, parenting manuals suggest offering two choices of appropriate outfits: "The blue jumper or the red one?"

We have presented a sensible choice, but the toddler feels as though she has had some say.

This same principle can apply to food choices: "Weetabix or toast for breakfast?"

## Kitchen control

Young children cannot make complex decisions. They have not yet developed the necessary skills and abilities.

If we throw open the kitchen cupboard and ask a child what she would like for tea or breakfast, it is confusing. She cannot yet weigh up multiple choices (and has no concept of the meaning of 'healthy'). The answer will, therefore, usually be the same as yesterday; or something which appeals to appetite alone, which is usually unhealthy ("What do you want for breakfast?" "Coco pops!").

You then have to defy this answer, quashing her choice ("No, you can't have that, it's not good for you,") which results in a tantrum.

Far better to offer two choices, within your pre-defined limits, from the start. Toast or Weetabix?

## Choice, not debate

Offering a limited range of choices is not the same as trying to reason with your toddler.

She does not yet have advanced enough reasoning skills, nor the ability to store enough information about consequences and choices.

Trying to reason, e.g.:

*'You need to eat it to make your heart healthy'*

will just drag a meal out and increase everybody's anxiety. It also alerts your child to the fact that this mealtime or food matters a lot to you. This will raise the pressure on her and reduce the chance that she will eat.

## Let them help themselves

Another good way of allowing your child some control at mealtimes is by allowing her to help herself at the table.

In my blog, I describe living and studying in Greece, where families (at least back then) tended to eat together more often, sharing from the table. Although life, times and food habits are fast-changing, it is still common in Greece for families and friends to share food from the centre of the table.

I think it is a great shame that we no longer bring food to the table for everyone to help themselves, instead of relying so heavily on portion sizes determined by food manufacturers. It takes away our ability to judge how much to put on our plate based on our appetite; instead, we eat pre-determined amounts and can be left overstuffed or unsatisfied.

So, bring back the centre dishes! With a little help, your child will take great pride in dishing out as much as she wants before handing it on.

## The vital choices

The very best way of allowing your child to exert some control at the dinner table is by allowing her choice over how much she eats – and by not trying to coax her into eating more when she is full.

If you do bring food to the table and allow your child to help herself, don't force her to finish what she has taken, or make her feel bad for being 'wasteful'. With practice, she will learn to judge her appetite soon enough.

A child should be allowed to decide how much to eat, and even to refuse to eat at all.

Don't fall into the trap of cajoling your child to eat just a bit more, just one more mouthful, or to just finish everything on her plate… and *then* she can have a sweet, or get down from the table, or be labelled a good girl. Allow her to eat as much as she needs.

If we try to get children to eat more than their appetites dictate that they need, they will grow up having learnt to eat a set amount, or whatever is on the plate. It is *much* better if your child can learn to eat to her appetite.

Didn't eat as much as she needed at this meal? Don't worry, that's OK – she will make it up at the next meal.

Which brings us to the last point: allowing your child to decide whether to eat at all. This probably has less to do with listening to appetite and more to do with allowing your child to exert her autonomy.

Have you noticed how, if you try and coax or cajole your child to finish that last little bit, she becomes even more willful and stubborn? You may then resort to some sort of bribe that only you, as a parent, have control over, such as getting a treat or being allowed to do something.

This doesn't allow your child the opportunity to practice decision-making, and to have some personal power. The lack of these opportunities will usually result in more difficult behaviour to follow.

## Day 25: Try this at home

Research has shown that being involved in preparing a meal or snack decreases fussy or picky eating, possibly by giving children a sense of ownership and pride[5].

Below, I have provided a list of some ways that parents have found helpful to give children a sense of control at mealtimes, without the little ones taking *all* the control.

See which ones might work for your family. Add any others that you can think of.

You could even let me know your ideas through my website (*www.fussyaboutfood.com*) – I'll be sure to include readers' ideas in future blog posts on the topic.

| |
|---|
| • Helping prepare the meal |
| • Helping set the table |
| • Telling other family members that it is time to eat |
| • Sitting at the main meal table with adults |
| • Helping themselves and putting food on their own plate |
| • Passing bowls/food/drink to others |
| • If served, deciding whether to have some of each of the foods on offer |
| • If served, and having decided to have some of the food on offer, deciding how much to have put on the plate |
| • Deciding where any served food should be put on the plate |
| • Eating for themselves, using cutlery and plates/ bowls that make this easier |
| • Drinking from an open cup like the grown-ups |
| • |
| • |
| • |
| • |
| • |
| • |
| • |
| • |

# Day 26: Portion Sizes

I often encounter parents who worry that their picky child is not eating enough.

Many parents tell me initially that they don't know what a portion size for a young child looks like, or that they give their child the same amount as an adult. Some parents resort to giving their child junk-type food in an attempt to get him to eat enough or to eat anything at all. Many parents admit to putting quite a lot of food on the child's plate, in the hope that he will eat just a little bit of something.

The result of all this is often that the child becomes even pickier and eats less. Parents then resort to convenience foods in an attempt to get him to eat.

A 2016 survey of 1,000 mums and dads by The Infant and Toddler Forum in the UK revealed that, while 79% of parents give their toddlers more than they need at mealtimes, 73% of mums and dads worry that their child is not eating enough[1].

## Why does this happen?

One factor is the change in adult portion sizes over the years. As our own portion sizes have got bigger, so have our expectations of how much children should eat.

Another problem is modern plate sizes. Plates have got bigger, and are less likely to have a rim, so our portions have grown to match.

## Trust their appetites

Young children are great judges of their energy needs. They tend to eat just as much as they need.

They do not follow the usual social norms of finishing the food on the plate but instead eat until they have had enough. This was demonstrated by researchers at the Pennsylvania State University in the US in 2000[2], who wanted to test whether younger children and older children eat more if they are served a larger portion size.

We know that, as adults, we *do* eat more if we are served larger portion sizes. In the world of nutritional research, we say that adults respond to 'visual cues' – the bigger the plate or the packet, the more likely we are to eat a larger portion.

In the Pennsylvania study, 32 children (16 were 3-year-olds; the other 16 were 5-year-olds) were given different sized portions of macaroni cheese on different days. The researchers weighed how much the children ate and how much they left. They discovered that the 3-year-old children did not eat more if they were served more. The amount the children ate was the same across all three days.

### What does this mean for the parent of a fussy eater?

Serving up larger portion sizes will not encourage your child to eat more.

Many parents tell me that they dish up more food in the hope that their child will eat more than he would otherwise. The research suggests that this is just not the case.

In my experience, and that of the many parents I have worked with, serving up larger portion sizes to young children just puts them off. The parenting worker I partnered with tells parents that large portion sizes seem unachievable to a young child – and the child *wants* to achieve. If the end goal seems unreachable, he will often give up before even starting, by playing up at the dinner table and refusing to try anything.

### What about the 5-year-olds in the study?

The older children in the Pennsylvania study *did* respond to larger portion sizes, eating more when they were served larger portions of macaroni cheese.

It is now generally accepted that, although younger children eat as much as they need, older children can learn to eat more than they need[3]. This is why it is so important to offer realistic and appropriate portion sizes to children, regardless of age. Otherwise, they will learn to eat more than is needed, which can contribute to obesity later in life.

I am going out on a bit of a limb here, but my observation from working with families is that this information is particularly relevant for dads and other male carers. It is probably because men need (and thus eat) more calories per day than women, and so their judgement of the right amount of food for a child can be skewed.

Although adult males, on average, *do* need more calories than adult females, the sex difference does not apply in the same way for young children: boys' and girls' energy needs are broadly the same per kg of body weight.

### Don't panic

Generally, healthy children will eat as much as they need to keep growing and to remain on their centile line. My own experience is that picky eaters have sometimes even gone *up* a weight centile.

Remember that children's appetites vary each day. Children are, I have often observed, much better at regulating their appetites than adults are.

We (as grown-ups) learn to eat set amounts at mealtimes. This is often through habit, or because foods are packaged in a certain way (a packet of crisps and a sandwich in a box). We have also prepared and paid for the food, of course, and most of us hate waste.

Children are probably much better than adults at listening to their appetite, eating only as required to satisfy their hunger.

## What is an appropriate portion size?

I often use a simple visual guide: A child's stomach is about the size of his loosely clenched fist.

This isn't, you will note, a lot of food!

I find the "hand model" portion guides the most helpful for families. It saves memorising charts and tables. Plus, you always have your hands with you. Researchers at the University of Sydney have shown that using your hands is more accurate than estimating the weight of foods using household measures, such as cups[4].

I particularly like the hand portion guide produced by the Dairy Council of California (see their website *www.healthyeating.org)* and download a printable guide for free at *bit.ly/FussyDay26a*, as it includes appropriate portion sizes of milk.

DAIRY COUNCIL of CALIFORNIA

# Serving-Size Chart

| FOOD | SYMBOL | COMPARISON | SERVING SIZE |
|---|---|---|---|
| **Dairy: Milk, Yogurt, Cheese** | | | |
| Cheese (string cheese) | | Pointer finger | 1½ ounces |
| Milk and yogurt (glass of milk) | | One fist | 1 cup |
| **Vegetables** | | | |
| Cooked carrots | | One fist | 1 cup |
| Salad (bowl of salad) | | Two fists | 2 cups |
| **Fruits** | | | |
| Apple | | One fist | 1 medium |
| Canned peaches | | One fist | 1 cup |
| **Grains: Breads, Cereals, Pasta** | | | |
| Dry cereal (bowl of cereal) | | One fist | 1 cup |
| Noodles, rice, oatmeal (bowl of noodles) | | Handful | ½ cup |
| Slice of whole-wheat bread | | Flat hand | 1 slice |
| **Protein: Meat, Beans, Nuts** | | | |
| Chicken, beef, fish, pork (chicken breast) | | Palm | 3 ounces |
| Peanut butter (spoon of peanut butter) | | Thumb | 1 tablespoon |

HealthyEating.org

*Dairy Council of California Serving-Size Chart*

*www.healthyeating.org*

The Infant and Toddler Forum produce an excellent booklet of appropriate portion sizes for 1-4-year-olds. It includes staple foods, meals, and occasional foods[5].

I have yet to find a resource that includes appropriate portion sizes of occasional (treat) foods which is relevant for every age group.

**Appetite evolution**

Remember that a child's appetite will vary depending on the child, how active he is, and the day.

Some children may need slightly larger portions than those described on Day 5 of this book and in the Infant and Toddler Forum guide. Others will need a little less. Your child's appetite is the best gauge.

Just try not to serve up too much and expect him to finish the food if it is more than his appetite requires. It is better to offer up small portion sizes (or let him help himself), perhaps on smaller plates. If he wants more, then he can ask for more.

Give children lots of praise for eating and let them continue to listen to their own appetites and eat just the right amount.

Letting children grow up aware of their appetites and feelings of fullness is probably one of the greatest gifts we can give a child. Just ask any adult who was made to clean their plate how they do today with stopping when full. Unless they have made a conscious attempt to become more mindful around food, chances are they still feel compelled to clean their plate, regardless of how full they feel.

**In summary...**

My advice regarding portion sizes can be summarised in three points:

1. Serve up appropriate portion sizes for children.

2. If they finish, let them ask for more if they want. Or you can ask, without expectation, if they would like some more. You might want to wait a short while before offering a second helping because it may take a little time for their stomach to register that it is in fact full.
3. Respect your child's appetite and let him grow up respecting his own appetite and feelings of satiety, fullness and hunger.

## Day 26: Try this at home

Download the Infant and Toddler Forum portion guide here: *bit.ly/Fussy-Day26b.*

Use the guide to tot up the size of one or two of your child's meals or foods. You can use the portion guide on Day 5 of this book if you prefer.

Use the table below to compare or keep a note somewhere else. You could even use your phone to photograph your child's meals and snacks and then compare.

| Meal or snack | Food or drink | Recommended serving | How did our serving compare? |
|---|---|---|---|
| Breakfast | Cereal | 3-6 heaped dessert spoons (2-4 US table-spoons) | I served up ½ bowl, so probably too much. |
| Breakfast | Milk | 1 cup of milk (100 – 120 ml / 3 – 4oz) | About right. |
| Snack | Diluted fruit juice | 100-120ml / 3-4oz | Our cup was about 2/3 full, so probably too much. |
| | | | |
| | | | |
| | | | |

What did this exercise reveal? Any surprises? Or reassurance that what you are serving up is about right?

# Day 27: Food Chaining

As young children learn what is good to eat, and what is potentially poisonous or dangerous, they put foods into different categories. You may remember categorisation from Day 10.

When a child experiences a new food, she will categorise it. The group will be based on its appearance, the food's name, and how closely it compares to foods that she already likes or dislikes.

Appearance includes things like colour and shape. If the food looks like something she already likes, then she is more likely to mentally put it in the category of 'liked food'.

Categorising new things based on prior experience is something that we all do, usually sub-consciously. It helps to give us a quick idea of what this new thing is and how to approach it.

## Food chaining

Whether your child puts a new food into the category of liked or disliked foods depends in part on how your child has experienced foods in the same category (e.g. 'Green Vegetables') in the past.

Was she ill after eating other foods in the same category? Did being presented with foods in that category result in negative pressure to eat them? If so, then it is very likely that this new food will automatically be put in the 'disliked food' category.

If, on the other hand, she had a positive experience with a similar food – it tasted yummy and she was praised for trying it – she is more likely to put the new food into the same 'liked' category.

This is the principle behind a process known as 'food chaining', which we will explore in detail below.

In short, you put the foods that your child already likes and enjoys into different categories. You then stretch the number of foods in each category by adding new foods that are *similar to already liked foods.*

Food chaining was developed by Cheri Fraker, a Speech and Language Therapist/Pathologist in Illinois, US. The technique was a response to treating an eleven-year-old who ate nothing but peanut butter, bread and milk. If you are interested in reading more about food chaining, I recommend the book written by Fraker and her colleagues: *Food Chaining: The Proven 6-Step Plan to Stop Picky Eating, Solve Feeding Problems, and Expand Your Child's Diet*[1].

The reason food chaining works is probably linked to familiarity, along with other ways children learn to like new foods. We looked at familiarity and "learning to like" in some detail on Days 11 and 13.

## Step 1: Categorise

You start by putting your child's foods into one of three categories:

1. The foods your child **currently** likes and eats (called the 'core diet')
2. The foods your child **used to** like and eat (but now does not like or eat)
3. The foods that your child has **never** eaten or liked

I have found it helpful to split the third group in two, so:

3. The foods that she has **never** eaten or liked

    a) Foods your child has never **liked**

    b) Foods your child has never **tried**

This is because it might be easier, using the principles of this book, to introduce completely new foods. The foods with which your child has had a negative experience could be more of a challenge (although still doable!).

### Step 2: Map

The next step is to "map" the foods that your child currently eats and likes by considering their sensory properties.

Put the already-liked foods into different groups using the following criteria:

- Shape

(e.g. round, long, square, big, small)

- Taste

(e.g. sweet, salty, sour, bitter, spicy, bland, sharp, hot, zesty)

- Texture

(e.g. soft, crunchy, chewy, smooth, lumpy, runny)

- Temperature

(e.g. hot, warm, cool, cold, icy/freezing)

- Colour

(e.g. red, yellow, purple, beige, white, clear)

### Step 3: Chain

Starting with a food your child already likes and eats, create a food "chain", extending from the already-liked item to a target food. Do this by changing just *one thing at a time* in the chain.

For example, your child might eat only a certain brand of frozen chicken nuggets, and you want her to enjoy homemade chicken nuggets and/or eat fish cakes.

So, if your child will only eat a certain brand of chicken nuggets along with frozen chips, you could focus on extending the chicken nuggets to fishcakes. Or you could focus on extending the chips to include vegetable fries. Or you could extend the chips to include other potatoes.

Either way, you should only change one food, and one characteristic, at a time.

Usually, we change first the shape, then the taste, and lastly the texture.

### Bonus ideas

- You can also offer a new food with already-liked foods, encouraging alternating bites.
- Parents should always focus on describing the features of the food, rather than encouraging the child to take a bite. This might sound something like: "Hmmm, this fishcake tastes, well, fishier, than the fish finger we made yesterday. But the ketchup with it makes it taste sort of sweet." This may pique curiosity.
- Finally, you can use something called "flavour masking" to encourage your child to progress along a chain. Flavour masking refers to using either a sauce (a 'wet' mask); or a spice, sugar or another dry condiment (a 'dry' mask) to transition your child from one texture or food to another. You simply offer the mask for her to dip the food in, or to sprinkle on. Dipping has been shown to increase supertaster children's intake of vegetables[2].

**Example food chain**

A food chain extending a child's diet from a certain brand of frozen chicken nuggets to fishcakes might look something like this:

Selected brand of frozen chicken nuggets

↓

A different brand of frozen chicken nuggets

↓

Homemade chicken nuggets

↓

Homemade breaded chicken strips

↓

Homemade breaded fish fingers

↓

Homemade breaded fish cakes

↓

Homemade fish cakes without breading

In the example chain above, you might be able to go straight from a different brand of frozen chicken nuggets to homemade chicken nuggets, however they come.

You might find that your child is much more sensitive and needs a more gradual change. In this case, you could start by making nuggets from minced chicken into the same shape as the frozen nuggets and using the same breading as the already-liked chicken nuggets. Then you could change *one thing at a time*, following the shape-first-then-taste-then-texture sequence.

For example, you could start by making the chicken nuggets into a different shape or different shapes. Next time, you could use chicken strips instead of minced chicken. The time after that, you could change the coating. If your child has accepted a smooth coating so far, try a breadcrumb coating instead.

You could also use tomato ketchup to mask, eventually 'fading' the flavour mask. The chain might then look something like this:

Selected brand of frozen chicken nuggets

↓

Selected brand of chicken nuggets with ketchup on the side to dip into

↓

A different brand of frozen chicken nuggets with ketchup on the side to dip into

↓

Homemade chicken nuggets with ketchup on the side to dip into

↓

Homemade breaded chicken strips with ketchup on the side to dip into

↓

Homemade breaded fish fingers with ketchup on the side to dip into

↓

Homemade breaded fish cakes with ketchup on the side to dip into

↓

Homemade fish cakes without breading with ketchup on the side to dip into

↓

Homemade fish cakes without breading and with BBQ sauce to dip into

↓

Homemade fish cakes without breading and with tartare sauce or mayonnaise to dip into

↓

Homemade fish cakes without breading and without sauce

This second chain might seem like a long one, but you have got all the way from a selected brand of chicken nuggets to fish cakes without sauce, which is great progress. You will probably not want to take a step along the chain every day, but you may have one or two other food chains to use on the other days.

You could fade out the flavour mask towards the end of the chain by offering a smaller amount of ketchup or other sauce. This will mean that the last few bites will have to be eaten without masking, as there will be no ketchup left. Alternatively, your child might assess the ketchup situation and work out that there is not enough; in which case, she might dunk a little less with each mouthful to make it last.

Alternatively, she might beg you for more or refuse to eat the last mouthfuls. If she begs for more, you must stand firm and tell her that there isn't any more and then get on with your own meal and change the topic of conversation. You might help her along at the beginning of the meal by saying that there is only a little bit of ketchup today. If she refuses to finish the fish cakes without ketchup, don't make a fuss or get angry or disappointed. Praise her for doing so well and finish your own food without asking her to eat up.

When you are done, clear the table and your child's plate, throwing away any leftovers. Meal over.

## The rating scale

A key part of food chaining is using a rating scale.

The rating scale is used to assess if, and how much, your child liked each step of the chain and each new food.

The rating scale is usually numbered 1-10.

The bottom of the scale (number 1) is a new food that your child definitely does not like.

The top of the scale (number 10) is a food that your child likes very much.

For younger children, parents rate their child's reaction. For older children, the children can rate their liking of the food themselves.

The rating scale helps to determine where to go with new food chains. Using the example chain above: If your child rated the tomato ketchup highly, this might suggest that you could either:

1. Use tomato ketchup to mask other new flavours initially, **or**
2. Try other sauces with a similar consistency to add variety to flavours (BBQ sauce, Thousand Island, Ranch-style dressing, etc.), **or**
3. Extend a tomato chain – for example, dipping pasta shapes into tomato ketchup, then dipping pasta shapes into tomato pasta sauce, etc.

## Day 27: Try this at home

I have found it helpful to first list all the foods a child enjoys, as detailed above.

We then take five different pieces of paper or card. Each piece represents one of the properties that I used at the beginning of this chapter (shape, taste, temperature, texture, colour).

Write the name of a food on each piece of card (the same food on each). Under the food name, write a description of the food's corresponding characteristic.

For example, one little boy liked plain penne pasta shapes.

Plain penne pasta shapes are:

- Long (shape)
- Bland (taste)
- Soft (texture)
- Warm (temperature)
- Beige or white (colour)

So, the cards might look like this:

| SHAPE | TASTE | TEXTURE | TEMPERATURE | COLOUR |
|---|---|---|---|---|
| **Plain penne** | **Plain penne** | **Plain penne** | **Plain penne** | **Plain penne** |
| Long | Bland | Soft | Warm | Beige/white |

On a big piece of paper, we draw a circle for each of the properties and its possibilities described above (for example, for temperature: hot, warm, cool, cold, icy/ freezing).

Finally, we go through each already-liked food, one at a time, and put it into one circle for each property.

If your child is old enough to understand, you could do this exercise together. You might split the exercise into several parts and do one each day to avoid your child getting bored with the exercise.

## Finding patterns

What you will start to notice is that several of the circles start to fill up. For example, you might notice that your child likes mostly warm foods or cold foods. They might like mostly soft foods or crunchy foods.

Noticing these patterns can help tell you where to go first with your food chains. Say, for example, your child likes mostly crunchy textures. They live on crisps and will not entertain bread. Your chain might, therefore, stick with crunchy textures to start with – something like this:

Crackers that are the size and shape of crisps

↓

Whole crackers, broken in half

↓

A different type of cracker broken in half

↓

The same cracker served whole

↓

The same cracker, served whole, with a flavour mask (like butter or jam)

↓

Well-toasted bread cut into the same size pieces as the cracker and with the flavour mask

↓

Lightly toasted bread served with the flavour mask

↓

A piece of bread, cut into the same shape as before, served with the flavour mask

↓

A piece of bread, cut into the same shape as before, served with a different flavour mask

↓

A piece of bread, cut into the same shape as before, served without the flavour mask

Have a go at starting a food chain with your child.

- What did you notice?
- Did you use a flavour mask?
    - If this mask worked well, could you use it again?
- Which aspects of a food's properties worked well for your child?
    - Texture?
    - Temperature?
    - Taste properties?
- How could you transfer what you have learnt from this exercise about your child's food preferences onto other food chains?
    - For example, did foods at a particular temperature work best?
    - Could you try new flavours, shapes and textures at the same temperature?

# Day 28: Children with Special Dietary Needs

Some children do have special dietary needs. Reasons for special dietary needs include:

- Food allergies
- Chewing or feeding difficulties
- Sensory issues
- Because they have received tube feeding in the past

There are several crucial periods in the development of a child's eating[1].

First is mastering the suck-swallow-breathe reflex, which fades at around 4 months old.

A baby will then learn different skills as feeding progresses, including:

- Moving food around their mouth
- Learning how to chew
- Co-ordinating their eyes, hands and mouth so they can look at the food, pick it up and put it in their mouth by themselves

For these skills to develop well, the nervous system needs sensory feedback – both from the food offered and how it is presented.

If taste, texture, and utensils used during this time do not change, a child does not learn to accept new foods – and therefore does not practice necessary new swallowing patterns[2].

Any illness during this time may delay progress, requiring a little more work and perseverance on the part of parents to establish good eating habits.

Babies who are ill and unable to eat or take milk for themselves during this period, and instead are fed through a tube, are often given "sham" feedings, so they can practice swallowing techniques and start to experience new tastes and textures. Sham feeding can help prevent problems later on.

I mention all this so that you can understand that if your toddler was ill for a prolonged time during the early developmental period, then he may have some food aversions that will take a little longer to resolve.

If he was offered very smooth-textured food during that time and was not able to practice with a variety of textures, getting used to different textures now may be a little harder. Note that I say, "a little harder," not "impossible". Most parents should not resign themselves to the idea that their child will always be difficult to feed.

Special dietary needs raise the risk that a child will have feeding problems[3]. Parents of children with special dietary needs can (understandably) be more anxious about their child eating well. This can sometimes mean that parents put pressure on him to eat, which nearly always means a child will eat less well[4]. Don't lose heart, though, because there is still a lot you can do to make mealtimes go more smoothly.

An in-depth discussion about strategies for managing food refusal in these particular situations is beyond the scope of this book, but I have included this one chapter on the topic to cover some more common situations where the risk of food refusal and picky eating can be heightened. These situations include children who have a food intolerance or a food allergy, and those who are not growing as expected (where medical opinion has ruled out a medical cause).

## Small children (or not growing as expected)

If a baby is small for his age, his mother is more likely to encourage and coax him to drink milk[5]. One could assume that the same will apply once that same child is on a solid diet.

---

Should you see a doctor first?

If your child is not growing as expected, or has dropped from their centile line, you must make an appointment to see a GP or other doctor.

This is because it is quite likely that your child has a medical[6], oromotor[7] (related to chewing and swallowing), or sensory[8] problem that the advice in this book will not be enough to resolve. The doctor may refer your child to a paediatrician, paediatric dietitian, speech and language therapist/pathologist, and maybe an occupational therapist.

Once you have followed through on the doctor's advice and taken up any referral appointments offered, then you can return to this book.

---

One of the first things that a paediatric dietitian will look at is where your child plotted on growth charts* when he was born, and how well he has grown since.

We looked at growth charts in some detail on Day 3. There, I explained that being small is not necessarily a bad thing. Some children are born smaller and some are larger. Providing feeding is going well and there is no underlying medical issue, then this is largely genetically determined.

* The UK-WHO growth charts in the UK. In the US and Australia, it's the WHO growth charts for infants and children aged 0 to 2 years, and the CDC growth charts for children aged 2 and older .

The important thing to look at is how well your child is growing. If he was born on the second centile for height and weight and has stayed on that centile line, then he is growing well; even if he will be smaller than many (or most) of his friends.

A doctor or dietitian will be more concerned if your child's height or weight drops below his expected centile line. There are many reasons your child's growth may have faltered; this is why it is important to tell your child's doctor if it happens.

If the doctor has ruled out any medical causes and puts this down to a "behavioural" issue, then it is worth thinking back over your child's feeding history.

### When did the problems begin?

In my experience, problems often start when a child (who was otherwise a fair eater) became unwell. This might have been a viral illness, a stomach illness, or even a series of urinary tract infections.

Because the child was unwell, he ate less. The child may have been small to start with and was now getting less nourishment. This often makes parents extremely anxious, and quite rightly so – feeding and nourishing your child is imperative.

Where things can go off track is when parents start to become anxious and put pressure on the child at mealtimes. The child senses this and eats less well. This causes even more anxiety for parents, the child eats even less, and so on it goes.

Even a poorly child is clever enough to realise an opportunity to get sweet foods and processed snack foods, and sometimes lots of milk and juice too. Milk can be particularly comforting. The result is often a poor intake of iron and, over time, iron deficiency anaemia. We talked about the importance of iron and preventing anaemia on Day 9.

### Steps to take

In cases like the one I describe above, start by applying the recommendations in this book.

- You may want to buy a multivitamin and mineral supplement for a short period (see Day 8).
- Make sure your child is offered foods that are nutritious with regards to iron, protein and fat. This will include red meat, other meat and fish foods, along with eggs, beans and pulses, chopped or ground nuts, or nut butter, cheese and butter or spread.
- Be careful offering too much milk and too many yoghurts, especially the very sweet children's yoghurts.
- Whatever you do, don't revert to baby foods, pureeing food, spoon-feeding your child, or any other feeding practice inappropriate for your child's age.
- You may want to fortify your child's diet for a short while. Fortifying simply means adding calories (and, often, protein). I include tips on food fortification in the Appendix.

## Weaning from a feeding tube

We do know that exposing a previously tube-fed child to tastes and textures can help wean him off the tube feed more successfully[9]; as long as the child's doctor, speech therapist/ pathologist or occupational therapist has said it is safe to do so.

We also know that being involved at mealtimes can help with the process[10]. The sensory elements (the sounds, smells and sight of food) and the social aspect are useful.

Painful experiences associated with eating can also contribute to food aversions. Humans learn to repeat behaviour by experiencing pleasurable feelings or sensations during or after an action or activity[11]. A child who has been fed through a tube may not have learned to associate eating with a good feeling (and therefore won't want to eat more).

If your child is weaning off a feeding tube, you should have the support of a multidisciplinary team. They will probably offer you and your toddler a programme which helps get him used to the sight, smell and touch of food.

- The programme might include activities that help your child become used to being touched on the face and around the mouth. These activities might also include "mouthing", which gets your child used to the sensory stimulation of having food in his mouth. Toys are often used for this.
- This work may also include exercises to help develop your child's oromotor skills, which are needed for chewing and swallowing.
- Any such programme might also include therapeutic tastes. These are tiny amounts of food used so that your child experiences the sensations of food, chewing, swallowing, tastes, and so on.
- You may also be advised to give your child sham feedings, to practice the swallowing techniques needed for eating and drinking and to start to experience new tastes and textures.

If you are in such a programme, you may still find many of the chapters in this book helpful. If in doubt, share this book with your child's therapy team.

If your child shows any signs of oromotor or swallowing difficulties, then you should speak to his GP or doctor. She may be able to refer him on to a Speech and Language Therapist/Pathologist and/or a physiotherapist for further assessment and an appropriate treatment plan.

## Swallowing difficulties

In the US, as many as 0.9% of children aged 3–17 have swallowing problems[12]. This can lead to feeding problems and food refusal.[13]

Addressing swallowing difficulties in children is a very specialist area and outside the scope of this book. Suffice me to say that if your child shows any of the symptoms below, you should take her to see her GP or doctor, as they might be a sign of swallowing problems:

- Coughing before or after swallowing
- Drooling, especially during meals
- Pocketing food inside the cheek
- Choking on certain foods
- Nose running or sneezing during or after a meal
- Trouble chewing
- Trouble swallowing liquids
- Trouble swallowing solids
- Taking a very long time to finish a meal
- Getting tired during the meal
- Refusal to eat certain foods or finish a meal
- A complaint of feeling like something is caught in the throat
- A gurgly voice during or after eating or drinking
- Throat clearing after a meal
- Repeated episodes of choking
- Frequent colds, pneumonia
- Unexplained weight loss
- Unexplained fevers that come and go

## Children with food allergies

Having a child with a food intolerance or allergy can naturally raise parents' anxiety about eating.

You have probably witnessed occasions when your child has been unwell, or even very ill, as a result of his allergy. You may have encountered accidental exposure from a food or meal that seemed safe. You may even have collected your child from a nursery or family member who unwittingly gave him something that made him unwell.

All of this will make you anxious. You will probably want to watch over him more at mealtimes. You are always on the lookout for signs of accidental exposure. You may have restricted the occasions that he eats with peers or other adults, to reduce the chances of this happening.

This precaution reduces risk, but the downside is that it also reduces the *opportunities* that your child has for watching role models eating.

Practically, feeding a child with a food allergy or intolerance often means making special meals and talking about food more than you would otherwise.

### Reducing the risk of pickiness

If your child has an allergy, it does not always mean that he will be unusually fussy with food.

One group of researchers that examined children under two years of age found that there was no association between food allergies and picky eating[14]; although another research group did find an association between picky eating for children and following a cow's milk protein-free diet.

This second group of researchers did, however, note that the most important factor in their findings of food pickiness was the total amount of prescription formula milk that the children drank[15]. As we saw on

Day 7, children who drink large amounts of milk or juice can be fussier, because they fill up on these instead of eating solid foods. This research might suggest that babies who have a cow's milk protein intolerance are no more likely to be fussy than their peers – *unless* they are given large amounts of formula milk.

The key is to reduce anxiety at mealtimes and to not make too much fuss over your child's eating; the same as for any other child. Too much extra fuss and your child will sense the pressure, as well as see an opportunity to give you the run-around and get alternatives.

Provide as many opportunities for role modelling, and for your child to eat, as you would for a child without intolerances. This will probably mean a bit more planning and meal preparation on your part.

It might be better to make more foods for everybody that your child can have, rather than have him eat different meals. This is likely to mean that the whole family will have to adapt to slightly different foods and meals.

Let's take an example. Your child has a Cow's Milk Protein Intolerance (CMPI). In planning a week's worth of family meals, this leaves you with three obvious choices:

1. Find meals that naturally do not contain cow's milk protein for the whole family to enjoy.
2. Adapt meals that the whole family enjoys so they do not contain cow's milk protein.
3. Your child has something different from the rest of the family (at some or all of his meals).

A different meal or snack can often be the safest option when you are out and about or eating when somebody else has prepared the food (e.g. at someone else's house).

Except for these occasions, you should probably choose a mix of options 1 and 2 – planning naturally cow's milk-protein-free meals for the whole family to enjoy and adapting family meals. This way, your child is not singled out, nor getting special treatment (both of which create expectations and pressure).

He also gets plenty of opportunities to watch role models enjoy the food he is also expected to eat.

### If a child is already picky

Follow the advice in this book, working through each day of the programme. For the most part, the child's needs regarding mealtime management and behaviour should not be very different from a child without a special dietary need.

Try as far as possible to take a matter-of-fact approach to your child's dietary restrictions.

- Don't let his restrictions mean that you prepare alternatives when food is refused or worry if he eats a little less one day.
- Don't force or bribe him to eat something.
- Don't feel guilty or sorry for him.

All this will lead to you making all sorts of exceptions, which will only lead to him eating less.

## Managing aversions

If a particular food has made a child ill in the past, chances are he will have developed an aversion to this food. This is particularly so for gastrointestinal illness – if the food made him vomit or retch[16].

If this is the case, continue to manage his food allergy as advised by his doctor or dietitian. Work on reducing food fussiness to other types of food and drinks.

Leave any food or drink that you think your child has developed a genuine aversion to until last. You can then use the principles of food chaining (described on Day 27) to gradually increase exposure to the food or foods that he has an aversion to.

Make sure that he is well when you do this, and therefore not likely to be gastrointestinally ill again.

## Good positioning for eating

Children need to be seated well to eat well – this helps with swallowing. When the pelvis is in a neutral position it supports the head. When the head is supported by the trunk, the tongue and jaw muscles aren't needed for support – and can instead be used for eating and drinking.

To make sure your child is seated well for eating and drinking, consider the following:

- Make sure your child is seated with 90 degrees at the hips, 90 degrees at the knees and 90 degrees at the ankles. Get down and have a look to see how your child is seated. Use a booster seat if necessary.
- Make sure her feet are supported. This is needed for core stability, which in turn is needed for jaw stability. Jaw stability is needed for tongue movement, chewing, and swallowing.
- Avoid "W" legs: when your child sits down with her feet pointing out to the side. A variation of this is wrapping her feet around the chair legs. Children and adults do this when core tone is low, as it provides more stability. Ideally, it is much better to practise upright sitting with her knees and ankles at 90 degrees. This allows better tone to develop, which means she no longer needs to grasp the chair legs with her feet for core support.
- Poor tone can lead a child to slide down in her seat. This affects head positioning and therefore also jaw stability. This will then affect tongue movement.

- You may need to strap your child in if she has poor posture. Ask a physiotherapist/physical therapist for advice if your child has postural issues.
- It can also help stability if your child has her arms resting on the arms of a chair.
- Poor posture can make a child wriggle at mealtimes. This is because she is trying to sit up and stay supported. This means she is focusing less on food and eating. It also makes the whole mealtime experience less pleasurable, both for your child and for you!

## Day 28: Try this at home

### Exercise 1: Eating posture

First, check out your child's posture for meals and snacks. Get down on all fours if it's necessary to be able to see properly.

- Are the hips, knees *and* ankles all at 90 degrees?
- Are the feet supported?

### Exercise 2: Recording meal similarity

Write down a few of your child's meals, snacks and drinks.

For the first part of the exercise, think about whether they differed from what everybody else was eating at the time.

Are there opportunities to make your child's meal or drink closer to everybody else's? For example, could you have had the same thing? Or could the meal or snack have been presented in a way to make it seem the same?

I have given you two examples so that you can see what I mean. One of these two children, Harry, has a cow's milk protein intolerance. His sister, Emily, does not.

| Meal | What my child ate |
|---|---|
| Breakfast | Weetabix with oat milk<br>Orange segments |
| Snack | Waffles and strawberries |
| | |
| | |
| | |
| | |

| Was this different from everybody else? | Could we make it closer to the same? |
|---|---|
| Emily and I had the same, but we both poured our own milk, whereas I gave Harry his in a bowl. | I could let Harry pour his own milk from the container if I put his out by him and keep an eye out that he doesn't try and use the milk we're using. Maybe I could use his milk too. |
| Emily had a shop-bought waffle that they both used to eat, but I made Harry a milk-free one. He fussed because he wanted Emily's, and then ended up breaking it apart and eating only the strawberries. | Maybe I could make milk-free ones for both of them, then he wouldn't be missing out. |
| | |
| | |
| | |
| | |

### Role models

Next, think about role models for each snack, meal or snack. Who did your child eat each meal and snack with?

Then think about whether this would have been different if they did not have an allergy. Are there safe ways for your child to experience more role models at mealtimes?

In the example above, Harry has most of his meals and snacks with Emily. So maybe Emily, who isn't particularly fussy, could have the same as Harry where foods need to be milk-free (like the waffles). In this scenario, I am making them for Harry anyway. Maybe I could have a waffle with them too? At breakfast, maybe I could have the same milk as Harry, or perhaps their father could be persuaded?

# Day 29: Reflux and Constipation

Some young children suffer from reflux and/or constipation. Both can reduce your child's appetite.

## Constipation

As many as 5-30% of young children will suffer from constipation at some point.[1]

Constipation can lead to food fussiness. In turn, food fussiness can lead to constipation if your child is not getting enough fibre in her diet.[2] It can become a vicious circle.

Fullness from constipation, slow stomach emptying, or discomfort from gastroesophageal reflux can affect the muscle contractions needed for swallowing. When this happens, tongue movement is affected and a child might continue to prefer puréed foods and other foods that do not need as much help from the tongue.[3]

There are several causes for constipation in young children – you should always consult your child's doctor or GP for advice and diagnosis.

The most common constipation in young children is idiopathic constipation – usually caused by a lack of fibre in a child's diet.

When your child first gets constipated, it can be painful or uncomfortable for her to open her bowels. She will then "hold" or try not to go to the toilet. This just makes constipation worse, as the stool is left inside the bowels, where it gets drier and harder.

> If you want to know more about constipation in children, including how to treat and prevent constipation, as well as toilet training, the ERIC children's bowel and bladder charity has some excellent resources.
>
> This includes information about good positioning for the toilet and a wonderful at-a-glance illustration. If you would like to know more, visit: *www.eric.org.uk*.

Over time, your child's back passage stays stretched and a signal is no longer sent to the brain to tell your child that she needs a poo. This can often mean that she goes to the toilet less and the stool becomes drier and harder still.

It can also mean your child doesn't know when she needs a poo, and so soils her underwear. Soiling and overflow diarrhoea are frequently signs of constipation.

The usual treatment for idiopathic childhood constipation in the UK at the time of writing is a macrogol based laxative[4]. This may need to be taken for several months. If this fails to work, then your child's GP or doctor might add a stimulant laxative such as sodium picosulphate, bisacodyl, senna or docusate sodium, depending on local arrangements. The doctor may also add or use lactulose, an osmotic laxative, instead – especially if the stimulant laxatives cause too much tummy ache, or your child's stools are very hard.

## Idiopathic constipation and diet

It is not recommended, at least in the UK, to treat idiopathic childhood constipation with diet alone.

But diet *can* help prevent further episodes in future.

If your child has been prescribed a laxative product, then you will probably have been advised to make sure she gets plenty of fluids, too.

Fluids help to keep the contents of our bowels moist, and easier to pass. If we are dehydrated, our bodies will draw fluid from our bowels and into our bloodstream. This is because we need enough fluid in our bloodstream to keep our blood pressure up and pumping to the brain. The body will always prioritise the brain – otherwise we would pass out!

## Reflux

Researchers have found a link between reflux and picky eating[5]. Reflux is one of the most common problems that make parents suspect a cow's milk protein intolerance in their child. As we have already learned, any gastrointestinal illness (like vomiting or reflux) increases the chance that your child will be fussy.

Children can suffer from reflux for a number of reasons and, like constipation, you should always consult your child's GP or doctor.

"Simple" or idiopathic gastro-oesophageal reflux is very common in babies, affecting as many as 40%. In 90% of cases, it resolves on its own before a child is 1 year old[6].

Reflux usually happens because a baby's food pipe (oesophagus) is still developing and the ring of muscle at the bottom of their oesophagus isn't yet fully developed. The ring of muscle (sphincter) at the bottom of the oesophagus is what helps to stop stomach contents leaking back out and up (reflux). The reflux we might experience as we get older is because this muscle becomes laxer.

Intolerance to cow's milk protein can be a cause of reflux[7] and your child's GP or doctor will consider this if your child does not respond well to first-line treatment.

## Day 29: Try this at home

Download the 'ERIC's Guide to Children's Bowel Problems' leaflet from the ERIC charity website, available from the following link: *bit.ly/FussyDay29*. Go to the second to last page ('How to get the poo in the loo!').

Is your child sitting in the right position when going to the loo?

- Are their feet supported and not dangling?
- Are their knees a bit higher than the hips?

# Day 30: Keep Going

Today is all about you.

There will be times when it can seem like a hard slog to keep going with meal planning and preparation; not to mention herding the family, getting them to eat together as often as possible.

You will need Oscar-award winning acting skills to remain calm and not pay attention to refusal when you are tired and fed up.

You'll probably have to negotiate with other family members and well-meaning friends with different ideas, who want to make your child sit at the table until finished, or who suggest offering bribes and treats in exchange for eating.

Then *I'm* asking you to do something completely different… and you even have a workbook to follow and fill in!

At times like these, you will probably ask yourself if the effort is really worth it.

*"Can't I just bribe or beg my child to eat three mouthfuls of each food at this one meal, and get it over and done with?"*

If you're feeling the strain, then stop – or at least slow down.

Don't rush to get through the days of this book, or to make any further changes for the next few days (or even a week or two) if you are struggling with a particular day of the programme. This is why the programme gives you the option to do a day over several days.

Most parents will start out wanting to steam on ahead, ploughing on towards enjoyable, stress-free meals as soon as possible. While this is completely understandable, most parents also do not expect the amount of work and effort needed to get there.

I never promised this was going to be easy!

If there were an easier way, then I promise I would have shared it. It would have made writing this book easier, too! If you have signed up for my newsletter or Facebook page, you'll get updates as I post them.

But, for now, the strategies in this book offer you the best chance for increasing the range of foods that your little one will eat; and for enjoying stress-free family meals.

## Day 30: Try this at home

Although today is the last day of the programme, there is still one last exercise to do.

Humans are really good at thinking about all that there is left to do. We are not so good at remembering how far we have come. This is called *negativity bias.*

To make sure that you remember how much things have changed, and so that you can appreciate all the hard work you have put in over the last few days, I have listed each day below and the key points from each one.

For each day, think about the changes you have made. Is there any work left to do, or are you satisfied that you have achieved as much as you can from this day?

As usual, I have given you an example.

Now is also the time to go online and complete the Child Eating Behaviour Questionnaire (CEBQ) for the third and final time at *fussyaboutfood.com/survey*. As before, if you are prompted for a code, then use *BOOK20*.

Once you have finished the programme (and completed the questionnaire three times throughout the programme), I will send you your results. Many are surprised to see how much things have changed from Day 1.

# P.s.

*If you enjoyed working through this book, and have seen positive changes, I would be very grateful if you could leave an honest review on Amazon or wherever you bought your copy. I personally read all of the reviews readers leave and do try and respond whenever I can.*

*I hope that you enjoyed this book and that you now enjoy mealtimes with your toddler. Follow me on my Facebook page 'Dr Elizabeth Roberts' or join my mailing list at www.fussyaboutfood.com for more updates. In the meantime, as the Greeks say:* Καλή όρεξη*! (Bon Appetit!)*

Dr Elizabeth Roberts

**Reviewing the programme**

| Day of the programme | Key points of the day |
|---|---|
| Day 2: Your own food history | • Thinking about my own relationship with food<br>• Thinking about how my own relationship with food affects how I approach my child's eating |
| Day 3: Children are very good at growing! | • Being reassured that my child is (most likely) growing just fine |
| Day 4: Do children need to eat differently from their parents? | • Am I giving my child lots of sugary or other snack foods because they will eat these? |
| Day 5: What children need to eat | • Checking out that my child is having enough of all of the food groups for good nutrition |
| Day 6: Mealtime routines | • Making sure that my child is offered 3 meals and 2 or 3 snacks at regular times (even if they do not eat them)<br>• Making sure that snacks are healthy and at scheduled times<br>• Avoiding distractions<br>• Limiting meal and snack times to 20-30 minutes |

| Do I feel this day is complete? | Is there still more work to be done? What more do we need to practise at home? |
|---|---|
| Yes/No | e.g. I still need to think about not expecting Harry to finish the food on his plate. |
| | |
| Yes/No | |
| Yes/No | |
| Yes/No | |
| Yes/No | |

| | |
|---|---|
| Day 7: Milk, juice and yoghurt | • Making sure that my child is not offered too much milk, juice, yoghurt or less healthy snack foods<br>• Making sure my child is no longer drinking from a bottle<br>• Making sure my child is not drinking (other than water) overnight |
| Day 8: Vitamins and minerals | • Making sure my child is getting enough vitamins and minerals |
| Day 9: Iron and iron deficiency anaemia | • Making sure that my child is getting enough iron |
| Day 10: Our natural food preferences | • Thinking about our natural food preferences and how we learn to enjoy new foods |
| Day 11: Learning to like | • Trying new foods without pressure |
| Day 12: Food neophobia – new foods from the perspective of a toddler | • Remembering that some fussiness is normal<br>• Thinking about how I/ us as parents have responded to our child's food refusal in the past |

| | |
|---|---|
| Yes/No | |
| Yes/No | |
| Yes/No | |
| Yes/No | |
| Yes/No | |
| Yes/No | |

| | |
|---|---|
| Day 13: Exposure | • Being exposed to new foods by having the food in the same room, smelling it, touching it, having the food on their plate, kissing the food, licking it and, finally, putting it in their mouth |
| Day 14: Repeated exposure | • Tasting without pressure<br>• Tiny Tastes |
| Day 15: Pressure to eat | • No cajoling, coaxing, begging or bribing<br>• Allowing my child to eat as much as they need |
| Day 17: Repeated exposure for your child with food-related anxiety or phobia | • Messy play<br>• Food-related activities without eating |
| Day 19: Boundaries and routines | • Being consistent |
| Day 20: Don't offer alternatives (and don't cater to your child) | • Not offering alternatives<br>• Not catering to my child |
| Day 21: Ignoring unwanted behaviour | • Ignoring food refusal behaviours<br>• Not offering food and snacks on demand |

| | |
|---|---|
| Yes/No | |
| Yes/No | |
| Yes/No | |
| Yes/No | |
| Yes/No | |
| Yes/No | |
| Yes/No | |

| | |
|---|---|
| Day 22: Giving effective praise | • Giving effective praise for desirable mealtimes behaviours |
| Day 23: Treats and bribes - managing behaviour with food | • Not offering treats for eating something else |
| Day 24: Role modelling | • Being a good role model |
| Day 25: Giving your child some control | • Giving my child an option of two<br>• Letting my child help themselves |
| Day 26: Portion sizes | • Offering appropriate portion sizes |
| Day 27: Food chaining | • Trying food chaining |
| Day 28: Children who have special dietary needs | • Taking the pressure off my child at mealtimes if they have special dietary needs<br>• Ensuring my child is sitting well at mealtimes |
| Day 29: Reflux and constipation | • Treating any constipation |

| | |
|---|---|
| Yes/No | |
| Yes/No | |
| Yes/No | |
| Yes/No | |
| Yes/No | |
| Yes/No | |
| Yes/No | |
| Yes/No | |

# About the Author

For several years, I have worked with families impacted by their children's fussy or picky eating.

I have talked to hundreds of parents who feel unable to feed their children despite having full cupboards. I have witnessed thousands of variances on a cocktail of anxiety, frustration and helplessness.

I have also spent a great deal of time poring through academic research on the topic of fussy eating in children. It became apparent that someone needed to organise the simple, actionable lessons hidden within these papers. Eventually, I realised that someone could be me. It would be impossible to speak to, and work with, these families without feeling moved to help in some way.

Aside from my work with families, what qualified me to take on this task?

I am a State Registered Dietitian in the UK. This means that I have had thorough training in food, diet, nutrition, and everything that goes with the topic. Throughout my career, I have worked with many different people and types of nutritional problems, both in adults and children. I often find common ground from one age range to another (for example, the evidence we will examine in the first chapter, about why we like sweet and snack foods, comes mainly from adult research – but it applies equally well to children).

I have also completed a PhD, which meant a good deal of research – and learning to be critical and inquisitive about the studies I have read. This time in academia also taught me how to sift through and organise large amounts of information and connect it in a way that is useful to people.

## Why did I write this book?

In 2015, I started working in Wales with families of children who were "picky eaters".

Starting out, I had no idea what to recommend families whose children simply would not eat the food that was offered. I knew what children *should* be eating, just not how to "get" them to eat it.

The purpose of the job was to help children and families to eat better. But how could parents improve their children's diets when the children simply wouldn't eat what had been prepared?

This conundrum set me off on a path of discovery. I wanted to find out why some children will just not eat some things, and what can be done about it.

First, I worked with a parenting expert and learned many of the strategies for managing food refusal from her. I also learned about the anxiety felt by parents when young children refuse to eat, and why this often leads parents to give their child anything that provides at least *some* nutrition.

Several years ago, I lived in Greece for a time. I looked after and taught young children for much of that time. When I began to tackle the "picky eater" problem, I was able to draw on my experiences of how mealtimes and feeding children are approached differently there. Some of these ways seem to work better, others less so.

Now, in the UK, I sifted through research papers and books on the topic and related subjects. I read about how both adults and children learn to like food – the chemistry, the science and the social and evolutionary reasons of how we learn to like (or dislike!) flavours, textures and foods in general. I discovered just how complex this learning process can be, and how modern living seems to have got in the way.

The parents I worked with had often been given limited exposure to new foods as children themselves and were, therefore, eating a limited range of foods. As children, they had their food cooked to order, were offered alternatives for refused food and given commercial snack foods, milk, and juice to compensate.

When it was time to feed their own toddler, they weren't sure what to do. They had no role model or frame of reference. How were they to know how to handle a fussy child? All their instincts told them to worry, fret and do whatever it took to get their child to eat.

I have worked with hundreds of families. I get so much joy from making the mealtime experience a pleasant one for each household.

Sometimes, parents found the science alone bolstered their confidence. They could understand why their child might be refusing food and what to do about it. It also stopped them blaming themselves or thinking that there might be something "wrong" with their child. Food refusal is part of normal childhood development, but modern lifestyles seem to make it worse and more taxing for parents than it needs to be. By changing how the parents managed and coped with food refusal, the families were able to eat a healthier diet.

## Sharing knowledge

As so many families were being referred to me for help, and other health professionals were asking for my advice, I realised that this is a wide-spread problem that lots of parents are struggling with.

I started a Facebook page, thinking that I could get all my views down on a blog post – but I soon realised there was much too much material for one post. So, I split the post up into several days. And then it spanned a few more.

That's where I came up with the idea to turn my research into a book with a topic and practical exercise for each day. I hope the information within this book has helped your family to enjoy less stressful meals and that your toddler is now trying a wider range of foods.

# Appendix: Fortifying your child's diet

If you find that your child has fallen off their weight centile line, or has special dietary needs making it harder for them to meet their calorie needs, then you might decide (or be advised), to fortify your child's diet; even if only for a short while.

Fortifying the diet really just means adding extra calories.

There are four ways that we get calories in our diet:

- Fat
- Carbohydrates (starches and sugars)
- Protein
- Alcohol (obviously not for children!)

Getting extra calories from protein alone is tricky, as these foods tend to come with fat.

Getting extra calories from starches can also be difficult, as they tend to fill us up.

We can, and do, get lots of calories from sugars – indeed, older people with a poor appetite may be told to try and include plenty of sugary foods in their diets. This is not advisable for children. This is partly because sugary foods lead to dental decay, but also because they (for the most part) do not add other nutrition, such as vitamins, minerals and essential fatty acids.

This leaves fats as the most effective way to add extra calories to the diet of a child struggling to maintain their weight.

So, the first port of call is to make sure that your child is having full-fat everything – and that your home cooking is full-fat. This means full-fat milk, thick and creamy yoghurts (not 'diet' or low fat), and no scrimping on oils, butter and cream in cooking. Make sure any spreads are not low-calorie options. Do try not to replace meals and snacks with milk though, as this will have an effect on iron intake (see Day 9).

Here are a few other ideas to try out, ordered by food groups:

## Dairy foods

- Try adding cheese to potatoes, salads, vegetables, etc.
- Add double cream to cereals, fruits, yoghurts, sauces, custards and puddings.
- Use full fat or thick and creamy yoghurts, fromage frais and crème fraiche as snacks, or add plain versions to foods.
- Add grated cheese to vegetables, potatoes, sauces, casseroles, omelettes, scrambled eggs.
- Cheese cubes or cheese on toast are a great high-calorie finger food snack.

## Protein foods

- Make sure you include a protein food with each main meal and at lunch – any type of meat, fish, poultry or eggs. For example, include minced meat, sausages, chicken, fish fingers or scrambled eggs.
- Eggs to dip with buttered soldiers, anything with cheese, or baked beans on buttered toast make an easy meal or snack.
- Try adding beans and other pulses like chickpeas and lentils to casseroles and curries.

## Fats and oils

- Spread butter or buttery spread thickly onto bread and any other bready or toasted foods, like crumpets or English muffins. Spread butter thickly on sandwiches, even if there is another filling.

- Use full-fat mayonnaise, salad cream and dressings for salads and sandwiches.
- Use oils in cooking wherever you can. For example, fry foods such as fish fingers, sausages, bacon, burgers, eggs and chips in sunflower, rapeseed (canola) or olive oil.
- Try adding a teaspoon or two of sunflower, rapeseed (canola) or olive oil to vegetables, pasta, potatoes, baked beans, casseroles and curries.
- Top food with cream sauces and dressing.

## High-energy snacks

- Offer a dessert after main courses such as trifles, sponges, mousse, yoghurt and ice-cream.
- You could try dried nuts, peanuts or trail mix for children over 5 years. For children of all ages, you could try peanut butter or other, milder nut butters on crackers or with apples.
- Try full-fat milkshakes.
- Mix full-fat yoghurts and fruit (fresh or canned) in a blender to make a refreshing yoghurt drink.

Other snacks ideas include:

  - A cake bar
  - 1-2 biscuits
  - A small bag of crisps
  - A cereal bar
  - Crumpets or scones with butter, jam or cheese
  - A muffin
  - Full fat yoghurt or fromage frais
  - Pepperoni sticks or slices. Slices may need to cut into half-moons for under-5s.

- Mini scotch eggs
- Mini sausage rolls
- Mini cheeses, like Babybel cheese or other miniatures
- Soft cheese triangles, Cheese Strings (string cheese), Cheese Dippers or Dunkers
- A buttered sandwich with jam, meat, fish, egg and mayonnaise, cheese or peanut butter

**Introduction**

1 Greer, F.R., Sicherer, S.H., Burks, A.W., 2008. Effects of early nutritional interventions on the development of atopic disease in infants and children: the role of maternal dietary restriction, breastfeeding, timing of introduction of complementary foods, and hydrolyzed formulas. *Pediatrics* 121(1), 183-91.

2 Jones, C.J. and Bryant-Waugh, R., 2013. The relationship between child-feeding problems and maternal mental health: a selective review. *Advances in Eating Disorders: Theory, Research and Practice*, 1(2), 119-133.

3 Mascola, A.J., Bryson, S.W., Agras, W.S., 2010. Picky eating during childhood: A longitudinal study to age 11-years. *Eating Behaviors* 11(4), 253–257.

4 Dubois, L., Farmer, A.P., Girard, M., Peterson K., 2007. Preschool children's eating behaviours are related to dietary adequacy and body weight. *European Journal of Clinical Nutrition* 61(7), 846-55.

5 Taylor, C.M., Wernimont, S.M., Northstone, K., Emmett, P.M., 2015. Picky/fussy eating in children: Review of definitions, assessment, prevalence and dietary intakes. *Appetite* 95, 349-59.

6 Steinsbekk, S., Bonneville-Roussy, A., Fildes, A., Llewellyn, C.H., Wichstrøm, L., 2017. Child and parent predictors of picky eating from preschool to school age. *International Journal of Behavioral Nutrition and Physical Activity* 14: 87.

7 Carruth, B.R., Ziegler, P.J., Gordon, A., Barr, S.I., 2004. Prevalence of picky eaters among infants and toddlers and caregivers' decisions about offering a new food. *Journal of the American Dietetic Association* 104(1 Suppl 1), s57-64.

8 Taylor, C.M., Northstone, K., Wernimont, S.M., Emmett, P.M., 2016. Macro- and micronutrient intakes in picky eaters: a cause for concern? *American Journal of Clinical Nutrition* 104(6), 1647-1656.

9 Chong Cole, N., An, R., Lee, S.-Y., Donovan, S.M., 2017. Correlates of picky eating and food neophobia in young children: a systematic review and meta-analysis. *Nutrition Reviews* 75(7), 516–532.

10 See for example: Lawless, J.W., Latham, M.C., Stephenson, L.S., Kinoti, S.N., Pertet, A.M., 1994. Iron supplementation improves appetite and growth in anemic Kenyan primary school children. *The Journal of Nutrition* 124(5),645-54; Stoltzfus, R.J., Chway, H.M., Montresor, A., Tielsch, J.M., Jape, J.K., Albonico, M., Savioli, L., 2004. Low Dose Daily Iron Supplementation Improves Iron Status and Appetite but Not Anemia, whereas Quarterly Anthelminthic Treatment Improves Growth, Appetite and Anemia in Zanzibari Preschool Children. *The Journal of Nutrition* 134(2), 348–356; Hambidge, K. M., Hambidge, C., Jacobs, M., Baum, J.D., 1972. Low Levels of Zinc in Hair, Anorexia, Poor Growth, and Hypogeusia in Children. *Pediatric Research* 6, 868–874; Shay, N.F., Mangian, H.F., 2000. Neurobiology of Zinc-Influenced Eating Behavior. *The Journal of Nutrition* 130(5), 1493S–1499S; Lawless, J.W., Latham, M.C., Stephenson, L.S., Kinoti, S.N., Pertet, A.M., 1994. Iron supplementation improves appetite and growth in anemic Kenyan primary school children. *The Journal of Nutrition* 124(5), 645-54.

11 See Lozoff, B., Corapci, F., Burden, M.J., Kaciroti, N., Angulo-Barroso, R., Sazawal, S., Black, M., 2012. Preschool-Aged Children with Iron Deficiency Anemia Show Altered Affect and Behavior. *The Journal of Nutrition* 137(3), 683–689; Georgieff, M.K., 2011. Long-term brain and behavioral consequences of early iron deficiency. *Nutrition Reviews* 69(1), S43-S48; East, P., Delker, E., Lozoff, B., Delva, J., Castillo, M., Gahagan, S., 2018. Associations Among Infant Iron Deficiency, Childhood Emotion and Attention Regulation, and Adolescent Problem Behaviors. *Child Development* 89(2), 593-608.

12 Ibid., 8.

13 Marchi, M., Cohen, P., 1990. Early childhood eating behaviors and adolescent eating disorders.*The Journal of the American Academy of Child and Adolescent Psychiatry* 29(1), 112-7.

14 Ünüsan, N., 2006. University students' food preference and practice now and during childhood. *Food Quality and Preference* 17(5), 362-368.

15 Van Tine, M.L., McNicholas, F., Safer, D.L., Agras, W.S., 2017. Follow-up of selective eaters from childhood to adulthood. *Eating Behaviors* 26, 61-65.

16 Nicklaus, S., Boggio, V., Chabanet, C., Issanchou, S., 2005._A prospective study of food variety seeking in childhood, adolescence and early adult life. *Appetite* 44(3), 289-97.

17 17 Ibid., 13.

18 Jacobi, C., Schmitz, G., Agras, W.S., 2008. Is picky eating an eating disorder? *International Journal of Eating Disorders* 41(7), 626-634.

19 Trofholz, A.C., Schulte, A.K., Berge, J.M., 2017. How parents describe picky eating and its impact on family meals: a qualitative analysis. *Appetite* 110, 36-43.

20 Sturm, L.A., Drotar, D., Laing, K., Zimet, G.D., 1997. Mothers' beliefs about the causes of infant growth deficiency: is there attributional bias? *Journal of Pediatric Psychology* 22(3), 329-44.

**Day 1**

1 Trofholz, A.C., Schulte, A.K., Berge, J.M., 2017. How parents describe picky eating and its impact on family meals: a qualitative analysis. *Appetite* 110, 36-43.

2 Van Tine, M.L., McNicholas, F., Safer, D.L., Agras, W.S., 2017. Follow-up of selective eaters from childhood to adulthood. *Eating Behaviors* 26, 61-65.

3 Cardona Cano, S., Tiemeier, H., Van Hoeken, D., Tharner, A., Jaddoe, V.W.V., Hofman, A., Verhulst, F.C., Hoek, H.W., 2015. Trajectories of picky eating during childhood: A general population study. *International Journal of Eating Disorders* 48(6), 570-579.

4 Dovey, T.M., Staples, P.A., Gibson, E.L., Halford, J.C., 2008. Food neophobia and 'picky/fussy' eating in children: a review. *Appetite* 50(2-3), 181-93.

5 Zucker, N., Copeland, W., Franz, L., Carpenter, K., Keeling, L., Angold, A., Egger, H., 2015. Psychological and Psychosocial Impairment in Preschoolers With Selective Eating. *Pediatrics* 136(3), e582-e590.

6 Lozoff, B., Corapci, F., Burden, M.J., Kaciroti, N., Angulo-Barroso, R., Sazawal, S., Black, M., 2012. Preschool-Aged Children with Iron Deficiency Anemia Show Altered Affect and Behavior. *The Journal of Nutrition* 137(3), 683–689.; Georgieff, M.K., 2011. Long-term brain and behavioral consequences of early iron deficiency. *Betsy Lozoff Nutrition Reviews* 69(1), S43-S48.

7 Van Rijn, I., Griffioen-Roose, S., de Graaf, C., Smeets, P. A. M., 2015. Neural Processing of Calories in Brain Reward Areas Can be Modulated by Reward Sensitivity. *Frontiers in Behavioral Neuroscience* 9, 371.

8 Mccormick, V., Markowitz, G., 2013. Picky eater or feeding disorder? Strategies for determining the difference. *Advance for NPs & PAs.* 4, 18-22, quiz 23.

9 This questionnaire was developed by the late Professor Jane Wardle and her colleagues at University College London (UCL) and can be downloaded from the UCL website. See, for example, Wardle, J., Guthrie, C.A., Sanderson, S., Rapoport, L., 2001. Development of the Children's Eating Behaviour Questionnaire. *Journal of Child Psychology and Psychiatry* 42(7), 963-70.

**Day 2**

1 Mura Paroche M., Caton S.J., Vereijken, C.M.J.L., Weenen, H., Houston-Price, C., 2017. How Infants and Young Children Learn About Food: A Systematic Review. *Frontiers in Psychology* 8, 1046.

2 Whitehouse, P.J., Harris, G., 1999. The inter-generational transmission of eating disorders. *European Eating Disorders Review* Corresponding Author
School of Psychology, University of Birmingham, Birmingham, B15 2TT, UK 6(4), 238-254.

**Day 3**

1 Fox, M.K., Reidy, K., Novak, T., Ziegler, P., 2006. Sources of energy and nutrients in the diets of infants and toddlers. *Journal of the American Dietetic Association* 106(1 Suppl 1), S28-42.

**Day 4**

1 Wilson, B., 2015. *First Bite: How We Learn to Eat.* London: Fourth Estate.

**Day 6**

1 Larsen, J.K., Hermans, R.C., Sleddens, E.F., Engels, R.C., Fisher, J.O., Kremers, S.P., 2015. How parental dietary behavior and food parenting practices affect children's dietary behavior. Interacting sources of influence?
*Appetite* 89, 246-57.

**Day 7**

1 Wright, C.M., Parkinson, K.N., Shipton, D., Drewett, R.F., 2007. How do toddler eating problems relate to their eating behavior, food preferences, and growth? *Pediatrics* 120(4), e1069-75.
2 Taylor, C.M., Wernimont, S.M., Northstone, K., Emmett, P.M., 2015. Picky/fussy eating in children: Review of definitions, assessment, prevalence and dietary intakes. *Appetite* 95, 349-59.
3 Harris, R.J., 2004. Nutrition in the 21st century: what is going wrong. *Archives of Diseases in Childhood* 89, 154-158.
4 Ibid.
5 Barbosa, C., Vasquez, S., Parada, M.A., Velez Gonzalez, J.C., Jackson, C., Yanez, N.D., Gelaye, B., Fitzpatrick, A.L., 2009. The relationship of bottle feeding and other sucking behaviors with speech disorder in Patagonian preschoolers. *BMC Pediatrics* 9, 66.
6 Satter, E., 2001. *Child of Mine: Feeding with Love and Good Sense.* 3rd sub edition. Boulder, CO: Bull Publishing Company.
7 Vanderhout, S. M., Birken, C.S., Parkin, P.C., Lebovic, G., Chen, Y., O'Connor, D.L., Maguire, J.L., TARGet Kids! Collaboration, 2016. Relation between milk-fat percentage, vitamin D, and BMI *z* score in early childhood. *The American Journal of Clinical Nutrition* 104(6), 1657–1664.

**Day 8**

1 Tharner, A., Jansen, P.W., Kiefte-de Jong, J.C., Moll, H.A.,van der Ende, J., Jaddoe, V.W.V., Hofman, A., Tiemeier, H., Franco, O.H., 2014. Toward an operative diagnosis of fussy/picky eating: a latent profile approach in a population-based cohort. *International Journal of Behavioral Nutrition and Physical Activity* 11, 14; Cardona Cano, S., Tiemeier, H., Van Hoeken, D., Tharner, A., Jaddoe, V.W., Hofman, A., Verhulst, F.C., Hoek, H.W., 2015. Trajectories of picky eating during childhood: A general population study. *International Journal of Eating Disorders* 48(6), 570-9; Chong Cole, N., An, R., Lee, S.-Y., Donovan, S.M., 2017. Correlates of picky eating and food neophobia in young children: a systematic review and meta-analysis. *Nutrition Reviews* 75(7), 516–532.

2 Carruth, B.R., Ziegler, P.J., Gordon, A., Barr, S.I., 2004. Prevalence of picky eaters among infants and toddlers and caregivers' decisions about offering a new food. *Journal of the American Dietetic Association* 104(1 Suppl 1), s57-64.

3 Taylor, C.M., Northstone, K., Wernimont, S.M., Emmett, P.M., 2016. Macro- and micronutrient intakes in picky eaters: a cause for concern? *American Journal of Clinical Nutrition* 104(6), 1647-1656.

4 Lawless, J.W., Latham, M.C., Stephenson, L.S., Kinoti, S.N., Pertet, A.M., 1994. Iron supplementation improves appetite and growth in anemic Kenyan primary school children. *The Journal of Nutrition* 124(5),645-54; Stoltzfus, R.J., Chway, H.M., Montresor, A., Tielsch, J.M., Jape, J.K., Albonico, M., Savioli, L., 2004. Low Dose Daily Iron Supplementation Improves Iron Status and Appetite but Not Anemia, whereas Quarterly Anthelminthic Treatment Improves Growth, Appetite and Anemia in Zanzibari Preschool Children. *The Journal of Nutrition* 134(2), 348–356; Hambidge, K. M., Hambidge, C., Jacobs, M., Baum, J.D., 1972. Low Levels of Zinc in Hair, Anorexia, Poor Growth, and Hypogeusia in Children. *Pediatric Research* 6, 868–874; Shay. N.F., Mangian, H.F., 2000. Neurobiology of Zinc-Influenced Eating Behavior. *The Journal of Nutrition* 130(5), 1493S–1499S.

5 Lozoff, B., Corapci, F., Burden, M.J., Kaciroti, N., Angulo-Barroso, R., Sazawal, S., Black, M., 2012. Preschool-Aged Children with Iron Deficiency Anemia Show Altered Affect and Behavior. *Journal of Nutrition* 137(3), 683–689; Georgieff, M.K., 2011. Long-term brain and behavioral consequences of early iron deficiency. *Nutrition Reviews* 69(1), S43-S48.

6 East, P., Delker, E., Lozoff, B., Delva, J., Castillo, M., Gahagan, S., 2018. Associations Among Infant Iron Deficiency, Childhood Emotion and Attention Regulation, and Adolescent Problem Behaviors. *Child Development* 89(2), 593-608.

7 Fox, M.K., Reidy, K., Novak, T., Ziegler, P., 2006. Sources of energy and nutrients in the diets of infants and toddlers. *Journal of the American Dietetic Association* 106(1 Suppl 1), S28-42; Chong Cole, N., An, R., Lee, S.-Y., Donovan, S.M., 2017. Correlates of picky eating and food neophobia in young children: a systematic review and meta-analysis. *Nutrition Reviews* 75(7), 516–532.

8 Sommerburg, O., Keunen, J.E.E., Bird, A.C., van Kuijk, F.J.M., 1998. Fruits and vegetables that are sources for lutein and zeaxanthin: the macular pigment in human eyes. *British Journal of Ophthalmology* 82, 907-910.
9 Public Health England, 2014. *National Diet and Nutrition Survey. Results from Years 5-6 (combined) of the Rolling Programme (2012/13 – 2013/14).* London: Public Health England.

**Day 9**

1 Harris, R.J., 2004. Nutrition in the 21st century: what is going wrong. *Archives of Diseases in Childhood* 89, 154-158.
2 Lozoff, B., Corapci, F., Burden, M.J., Kaciroti, N., Angulo-Barroso, R., Sazawal, S., Black, M., 2012. Preschool-Aged Children with Iron Deficiency Anemia Show Altered Affect and Behavior. *Journal of Nutrition* 137(3), 683–689; Moy, R.J., 2006. Prevalence, consequences and prevention of childhood nutritional iron deficiency: a child public health perspective. *Clinical & Laboratory Haematology* 28(5), 291-8; Booth, I.W., Aukett, M.A., 1997. Iron deficiency anaemia in infancy and early childhood. *Archives of Diseases in Childhood* 76(6), 549-53.
3 Burke, R.M., Leon, J.S., Suchdev, P.S., 2014. Identification, prevention and treatment of iron deficiency during the first 1000 days. *Nutrients* 6(10), 4093-114.
4 Ibid.
5 See for example: Beard, J., 2003. Iron deficiency alters brain development and functioning. *The Journal of Nutrition* 133(5 Suppl 1), 1468S-72S; Lozoff, B., 2011. Early iron deficiency has brain and behavior effects consistent with dopaminergic dysfunction. *The Journal of Nutrition* 141(4), 740S-746S.
6 WHO, 2011. *Haemoglobin concentrations for the diagnosis of anaemia and assessment of severity. Vitamin and Mineral Nutrition Information System* [online]. Geneva: World Health Organization; Scientific Advisory Committee on Nutrition, 2010. *Iron and health.* London: The Stationary Office.
7 McAdam, D.B., Sherman, J.A., Sheldon, J.B., Napolitano, D.A., 2004. Behavioral interventions to reduce the pica of persons with developmental disabilities. *Behavior Modification* 28(1), 45-72; Hagopian, L.P., Rooker, G.W., Rolider, N.U., 2011. Identifying empirically supported treatments for pica in individuals with intellectual disabilities. *Research in Developmental Disabilities* 32(6), 2114-20.
8 Public Health England, 2014. *National Diet and Nutrition Survey. Results from Years 1, 2, 3 and 4 (combined) of the Rolling Programme (2008/2009 – 2011/2012).* London: Public Health England.
9 Kaganov,B., Caroli, M., Mazur, A., Singhal, A., Vania, A., 2015. Suboptimal Micronutrient Intake among Children in Europe. *Nutrients* 7(5), 3524–3535.
10 Booth, I.W., Aukett, M.A., 1997. Iron deficiency anaemia in infancy and early childhood. *Archives of Diseases in Childhood* 76(6), 549-53.

11 Harris, R.J., 2004. Nutrition in the 21st century: what is going wrong. *Archives of Diseases in Childhood* 89, 154-158.

**Day 10**

1 Rozin, P., Fallon, A.E., 1987. A Perspective on Disgust. *Psychological Review* 94(1), 23-41.

2 See for example: Dovey, T.M., Staples, P.A., Gibson, E.L., Halford, J.C., 2008. Food neophobia and 'picky/fussy' eating in children: a review. *Appetite* 50(2-3), 181-93; Flight, I., Leppard, P., Cox, D.N., 2003. Food neophobia and associations with cultural diversity and socio-economic status amongst rural and urban Australian adolescents. *Appetite* 41(1), 51-9; Martins, Y., Pliner, P., 2005. Human food choices: an examination of the factors underlying acceptance/rejection of novel and familiar animal and nonanimal foods. *Appetite* 45(3), 214-24; Milton, K., 1993. Diet and primate evolution. *Scientific American* 269, 70–77; Russell, C.G., Worsley, A., 2008. A population-based study of preschoolers' food neophobia and its associations with food preferences. *Journal of Nutrition Education and Behavior* 40(1), 11-9.

3 See Addessi, E., Galloway, A.T., Visalberghi, E., Birch, L.L., 2005. Specific social influences on the acceptance of novel foods in 2-5-year-old children. *Appetite* 45(3), 264-71; Birch, L.L., Gunder, L., Grimm-Thomas, K., Laing, D.G., 1998. Infants' consumption of a new food enhances acceptance of similar foods. *Appetite* 30(3), 283-95; Rozin, P., Vollmecke, T.A., 1986. Food likes and dislikes. *Annual Review of Nutrition* 6, 433-56.

4 Cooke, L., Wardle, J., Gibson, E.L., 2003. Relationship between parental report of food neophobia and everyday food consumption in 2-6-year-old children. *Appetite* 41(2), 205-6.

5 Addessi, E., Visalberghi, E., 2006. How social influences affect food neophobia in captive chimpanzees: a comparative approach. *In*: Matsuzawa, T., Tomonaga, M., Tanaka, M., eds. *Cognitive Development in Chimpanzees*. Tokyo: Springer-Verlag, 246-264.

6 Birch, L.L., Doub, A.E., 2014. Learning to eat: birth to age 2 y. *The American Journal of Clinical Nutrition* 99(3), 723S-8S.

7 Mura Paroche, M., Caton, S.J., Vereijken, C.M.J.L., Weenen, H., Houston-Price, C., 2017. How infants and young children learn about food: a systematic review. *Frontiers in Psychology* 25(8), 1046.

8 Alexandra W. Logue, A. E., 2014. *The Psychology of Eating and Drinking*. Abingdon-on-Thames: Routledge.

9 Havermans, R.C., Jansen, A., 2007. Increasing children's liking of vegetables through flavour-flavour learning. *Appetite* 48(2), 259-62.

10 Maltodextrin is often added to savoury foods. Brain imaging studies have shown that, although humans cannot taste maltodextrin, it fires up the reward centre in our

brains (van Rijn, I., Griffioen-Roose, S., de Graaf, C., Smeets, P. A. M., 2015. Neural Processing of Calories in Brain Reward Areas Can be Modulated by Reward Sensitivity. *Frontiers in Behavioral Neuroscience* 9, 371). Check out the list of ingredients on some of your favourite moorish savoury snacks and see how many contain maltodextrin.
11 Chong Cole, N., An, R., Lee, S-Y., Sharon M Donovan, S.M., 2017. Correlates of picky eating and food neophobia in young children: a systematic review and meta-analysis. *Nutrition Reviews* 75(7), 516–532.
12 Kauer, J., Pelchat, M.L., Rozin, P., Zickgraf, H.F., 2015. Adult picky eating. Phenomenology, taste sensitivity, and psychological correlates. *Appetite* 90, 219-28.
13 See for example Gibson, E. L., Kreichauf, S., Wildgruber, A., Vögele, C., Summerbell, C.D., Nixon, C., Moore, H., Douthwaite, W., Manios, Y., 2012. A narrative review of psychological and educational strategies applied to young children's eating behaviours aimed at reducing obesity risk. *Obesity Reviews* 13(Suppl. 1), 85–95.
14 Kauer, J., Pelchat, M.L., Rozin, P., Zickgraf, H.F., 2015. Adult picky eating. Phenomenology, taste sensitivity, and psychological correlates. *Appetite* 90, 219-28.
15 Ibid.
16 Trabulsi, J.C., Mennella, J.A., 2012. Diet, sensitive periods in flavour learning, and growth. *International Review of Psychiatry* 24(3), 219-30.
17 Mura Paroche, M., Caton, S.J., Vereijken, C.M.J.L., Weenen, H., Houston-Price, C., 2017. How infants and young children learn about food: a systematic review. *Frontiers in Psychology* 25(8), 1046.

**Day 11**

1 BBC, 14 October 2016. Available from: www.bbc.co.uk/news/health-37642587 [Accessed 29 August 2017].
2 Smith, A.D., Herle, M., Fildes, A., Cooke, L., Steinsbekk, S., Llewellyn, C.H., 2017. Food fussiness and food neophobia share a common etiology in early childhood. *Journal of Child Psychology and Psychiatry* 58(2), 189-196.
3 Ibid.; 192.
4 Rozin, P., Haidt, J., & McCauley, C. R., 2008. Disgust. *In:* M. Lewis, J. M. Haviland-Jones, & L. F. Barrett eds. *Handbook of emotions.* New York: The Guilford Press, 757-776.
5 For a full discussion, see: Rozin, P. and Fallon, A.E., 1987. A perspective on disgust. *Psychological Review* 94(1), 23-41.
6 Batsell Jr., W.R., Brown, A.S., Ansfield, M.E., Paschall, G.Y., 2002. "You Will Eat All of That!": A retrospective analysis of forced consumption episodes. *Appetite* 38(3), 211-219.
7 Ibid., 5.

8 Havermans, R.C., Jansen, A., 2007. Increasing children's liking of vegetables through flavour-flavour learning. *Appetite* 48(2), 259-62.
9 Birch, L.L., Doub, A.E., 2014. Learning to eat: birth to age 2 y. *The American Journal of Clinical Nutrition* 99(3), 723S-8S.
10 Anzman-Frasca, S., Savage, J.S., Marini, M.E., Fisher, J.O., Birch, L.L., 2012. Repeated exposure and associative conditioning promote preschool children's liking of vegetables. *Appetite* 58(2), 543-53; Fisher, J.O., Mennella, J.A., Hughes, S.O., Liu, Y., Mendoza, P.M., Patrick, H., 2012. Offering "dip" promotes intake of a moderately-liked raw vegetable among preschoolers with genetic sensitivity to bitterness. *Journal of the Academy of Nutrition and Dietetics* 112(2), 235-45.
11 Paroche, M.M., Caton, S.J., Vereijken, C.M.J.L., Weenen, H., Houston-Price, C., 2017. How Infants and Young Children Learn About Food: A Systematic Review. *Frontiers in Psychology* 25(8), 1046.
12 Martins, Y., Pelchat, M.L., Pliner, P., 1997. "Try it; it's good and it's good for you": effects of taste and nutrition information on willingness to try novel foods. *Appetite* 28(2), 89-102; Pelchat, M.L., Pliner, P., 1995. "Try it. You'll like it." Effects of information on willingness to try novel foods. *Appetite* 24(2), 153-65; Birch, L., 1980. Effects of peers models food choice and eating behavior on preschoolers food preferences. *Child Development* 51, 489-496.

**Day 12**

1 Lafraire, J., Rioux, C., Giboreau, A., Picard, D., 2016. Food rejections in children: Cognitive and social/environmental factors involved in food neophobia and picky/fussy eating behavior. *Appetite* 96, 347-357.
2 Although some varieties of brussel sprouts on supermarket shelves have now been bred to have less of these bitter tasting compounds. There is a no longer an excuse to not enjoy them, even for PTC/PROP supertasters!
3 Alexandra W. Logue, A. E., 2014. *The Psychology of Eating and Drinking.* Abingdon-on-Thames: Routledge.
4 Supertasters also seem to reject foods that contain compounds that interfere with how we metabolise iodine (goitrogens). Iodine is essential for our thyroid glands, and is found naturally in seafood, seaweeds and in vegetables grown near the sea. Many hundreds of years ago, some populations living inland had very little iodine in their diets, resulting in goitres – swollen thyroid glands in the neck, sometimes quite large. These goitrogens are found in many of the green leafy vegetables, like watercress and 'greens', as well as in horseradish. It would have made sense to have a genetic drive to reject these foods in areas where there was very little iodine in the diet.
5 Ibid., 1.

6 van der Horst, K., Deming, D.M., Lesniauskas, R., Carr, B.T., Reidy, K.C., 2016. Picky eating: Associations with child eating characteristics and food intake. *Appetite* 103, 286-293.

7 Ibid.

8 Mura Paroche, M., Caton, S.J., Vereijken, C.M.J.L., Weenen, H., Houston-Price, C., 2017. How Infants and Young Children Learn About Food: A Systematic Review. *Frontiers in Psychology* 25(8), 1046.

9 Ibid.

10 Brown, S.D., Harris, G., Bell, L., Lines, L.M., 2012. Disliked food acting as a contaminant in a sample of young children. *Appetite* 58(3), 991-6.

**Day 13**

1 Mura Paroche, M., Caton, S.J., Vereijken, C.M.J.L., Weenen, H., Houston-Price, C., 2017. How Infants and Young Children Learn About Food: A Systematic Review. Frontiers in Psychology 25(8), 1046.

2 Birch, L.L., Gunder, L., Grimm-Thomas, K., Laing, D.G., 1998. Infants' consumption of a new food enhances acceptance of similar foods. Appetite 30(3), 283-95.

3 Bahar, A., Dudai, Y., Ahissar, E., 2004. Neural signature of taste familiarity in the gustatory cortex of the freely behaving rat. *Journal of Neurophysiology*. 92(6), 3298–308.

4 Ibid., 1.

5 Wardle, J., Herrera, M.L., Cooke, L., Gibson, E.L., 2003. Modifying children's food preferences: the effects of exposure and reward on acceptance of an unfamiliar vegetable. *European Journal of Clinical Nutrition* 57: 341–348.

6 Remy, E., Issanchou, S., Chabanet, C., Nicklaus, S., 2013. Repeated exposure of infants at complementary feeding to a vegetable puree increases acceptance as effectively as flavor-flavor learning and more effectively than flavor-nutrient learning. *The Journal of Nutrition* 143(7), 1194-200.

7 Wadhera, D., Capaldi Phillips, E.D., Wilkie, L.M.. 2015. Teaching children to like and eat vegetables. *Appetite* 93, 75-84.

8 Ibid., 2

9 Ibid., 1.

10 Ibid., 2.

11 Ibid., 1

12 Rolls, B.J., 1986. Sensory-specific satiety. *Nutrition Reviews* 44(3), 93-101.

13 Birch, L.L., McPhee, L., Shoba, B.C., Pirok, E., Steinberg, L., 1987. What kind of exposure reduces children's food neophobia? Looking vs. tasting. *Appetite* 9(3), 171-8.; Wardle, J., Carnell, S., Cooke, L., 2005. Parental control over feeding and children's fruit and vegetable intake: how are they related? The Journal of the American Dietetic

Association 105(2), 227-32; Wardle, J., Herrera, M.L., Cooke, L., Gibson, E.L., 2003. Modifying children's food preferences: the effects of exposure and reward on acceptance of an unfamiliar vegetable. The European Journal of Clinical Nutrition 57(2), 341-8.

14 Lundy, B., Field, T., Carraway, K., Hart, S., Malphurs, J., Rosenstein, M., Pelaez-Nogueras, M., Coletta, F., Ott, D., Hernandez-Reif, M., 1998. Food Texture Preferences in Infants Versus Toddlers. *Early Child Development and Care* 146(1), 69-85.

**Day 14**

1 Paroche, M.M., Caton, S.J., Vereijken, C.M.J.L., Weenen, H., Houston-Price, C., 2017. How Infants and Young Children Learn About Food: A Systematic Review. *Frontiers in Psychology* 8, 1046.

2 Cooke, L.J., Chambers, L.C., Añez, E.V., Wardle, J., 2011. Facilitating or undermining? The effect of reward on food acceptance. A narrative review. *Appetite* 57(2), 493-7.

3 Ibid., 1.

4 van der Horst, K., Deming, D.M., Lesniauskas, R., Carr, B.T., Reidy, K.C., 2016. Picky eating: Associations with child eating characteristics and food intake. *Appetite* 103, 286-293.

5 Satter, E., 2001. Child of Mine: *Feeding with Love and Good Sense.* 3rd sub edition. Boulder, CO: Bull Publishing Company.

**Day 15**

1 Larsen, J.K., Hermans, R.C., Sleddens, E.F., Engels, R.C., Fisher, J.O., Kremers, S.P., 2015. How parental dietary behavior and food parenting practices affect children's dietary behavior. Interacting sources of influence? *Appetite* 89, 246-57.

2 Wadhera, D., Capaldi Phillips, E.D., Wilkie, L.M.. 2015. Teaching children to like and eat vegetables. *Appetite* 93, 75-84.

3 Chong Cole, N., An, R., Lee, S.L., Donovan, S.M., 2017. Correlates of picky eating and food neophobia in young children: a systematic review and meta-analysis. *Nutrition Reviews* 75(7), 516–532.

4 Paroche, M.M., Caton, S.J., Vereijken, C.M.J.L., Weenen, H., Houston-Price, C., 2017. How Infants and Young Children Learn About Food: A Systematic Review. *Frontiers in Psychology* 8, 1046.

5 Dev, D. A., Speirs, K.E., Williams, N.A., Ramsay, S., McBride, B.A., Hatton-Bowers, H., 2017. Providers perspectives on self-regulation impact their use of responsive feeding practices in child care. *Appetite* 118, 66-74.

6 Satter, E., 2001. Child of Mine: *Feeding with Love and Good Sense.* 3rd sub edition. Boulder, CO: Bull Publishing Company.
7 Galloway, A.T., Fiorito, L.M., Francis, L.A., Birch, L.L., 2006. 'Finish your soup': counterproductive effects of pressuring children to eat on intake and affect. *Appetite* 46(3), 318-23.
8 Batsell W.R. Jr., Brown, A.S., 1998. Human Flavor-Aversion Learning: A Comparison of Traditional Aversions and Cognitive Aversions. *Learning and Motivation* 29(4), 383-396; Batsell, W.R. Jr., Brown, A.S., Ansfield, M.E., Paschall, G.Y., 2002. "You will eat all of that!": a retrospective analysis of forced consumption episodes. *Appetite* 38(3), 211-9.
9 Johnson, R., Harris, G., 2004. A preliminary study of the predictors of feeding problems in late infancy. *Journal of Reproductive and Infant Psychology* 22(3), 183-188; Cassells, E.L., Magarey, A.M., Daniels, L.A., Mallan, K.M., 2014. The influence of maternal infant feeding practices and beliefs on the expression of food neophobia in toddlers. *Appetite* 82, 36-42; Brown, A., Lee, M.D., 2015. Early influences on child satiety-responsiveness: the role of weaning style. *Pediatric Obesity* 10(1), 57-66.
10 Lumeng, J.C., Miller, A.L., Appugliese, D., Rosenblum, K., Kaciroti, N., 2018. Picky eating, pressuring feeding, and growth in toddlers. *Appetite* 123, 299-305.

**Day 16**

1 Grandin, T. 1992. Calming Effects of Deep Touch Pressure in Patients with Autistic Disorder, College Students, and Animals. *Journal Of Child And Adolescent Psychopharmacology* 2(1), 63-72.
2 Steinsbekk, S., Bonneville-Roussy, A., Fildes, A., Llewellyn, C.H., Wichstrøm, L., 2017. Child and parent predictors of picky eating from preschool to school age. *International Journal of Behavioral Nutrition and Physical Activity* 14, 87.

**Day 17**

1 Paroche, M.M., Caton, S.J., Vereijken, C.M.J.L., Weenen, H., Houston-Pric, C., 2017. How Infants and Young Children Learn About Food: A Systematic Review. *Frontiers in Psychology* 8, 1046.
2 Batsell, W.R. Jr., Brown, A.S., 1998. Human Flavor-Aversion Learning: A Comparison of Traditional Aversions and Cognitive Aversions. *Learning and Motivation* 29(4), 383-396; Batsell, W.R., Jr., Brown, A.S., Ansfield, M.E., Paschall, G.Y., 2002. "You Will Eat All of That!": A retrospective analysis of forced consumption episodes. *Appetite* 38(3), 211-219.

3 Ibid., 1.
4 Heath, P., Houston-Price, C., Kennedy, O.B., 2014. Let's look at leeks! Picture books increase toddlers' willingness to look at, taste and consume unfamiliar vegetables. *Frontiers in Psychology* 5, 191.

**Day 18**

1 Lafraire, J., Rioux, C., Giboreau, A., Picard, D., 2016. Food rejections in children: Cognitive and social/environmental factors involved in food neophobia and picky/ fussy eating behavior. *Appetite* 96, 347-357.
2 Coulthard, H., Thakker, D., 2015. Enjoyment of tactile play in preschool children is associated with food neophobia. *Journal of the Academy of Nutrition & Dietetics* 115(7), 1134-1140.
3 Steinsbekk, S., Bonneville-Roussy, A., Fildes, A., Llewellyn, C.H., Wichstrøm, L., 2017. Child and parent predictors of picky eating from preschool to school age. *International Journal of Behavioral Nutrition and Physical Activity* 14, 87.
4 Monnery-Patris, S., Wagner, S., Rigal, N., Schwartz, C., Chabanet, C., Issanchou, S., Nicklaus, S., 2015. Smell differential reactivity, but not taste differential reactivity, is related to food neophobia in toddlers. *Appetite* 95, 303-9.
5 See for example: Blissett, J., Harris, G., Kirk, J., 2001. Feeding problems in Silver-Russell syndrome.
*Developmental Medicine and Child Neurology* 43(1), 39-44.
6 Higashida, N., 2014. *The Reason I Jump: one boy's voice from the silence of autism.* London: Sceptre.
7 Mura Paroche M., Caton S.J., Vereijken, C.M.J.L., Weenen, H., Houston-Price, C., 2017. How Infants and Young Children Learn About Food: A Systematic Review. *Frontiers in Psychology* 8, 1046.
8 Rioux, C., Lafraire, J., Picard, D., 2018. Visual exposure and categorization performance positively influence 3- to 6-year-old children's willingness to taste unfamiliar vegetables. *Appetite* 120: 32-42.
9 Ibid.
10 Bartoshuk, L.M., 2000. Comparing sensory experiences across individuals: recent psychophysical advances illuminate genetic variation in taste perception. *Chemical Senses* 25(4), 447–460.
11 Törnwall, O., Silventoinen, K., Kaprio, J., Tuorila, H., 2012. Why do some like it hot? Genetic and environmental contributions to the pleasantness of oral pungency. *Physiology and Behavior* 107(3), 381-9.
12 Ibid., 10.
13 van der Horst, K., Deming, D.M., Lesniauskas, R., Carr, B.T., Reidy, K.C., 2016. Picky eating: Associations with child eating characteristics and food intake. *Appetite* 103, 286-293.

14 Ibid., 10.
15 Hayes, J.E., Duffy, V.B., 2007. Revisiting sugar-fat mixtures: sweetness and creaminess vary with phenotypic markers of oral sensation. *Chemical Senses* 32(3), 225-36.
16 Ibid., 10.
17 Daiyan, H., Campbell, C., Bartoshuk, L., Fillingim, R., 2008. Taste perception related to pain responses among African Americans and non-Hispanic whites. *Journal of Pain* 9, 62-62.
18 Pickering, G.J., Haverstock, G., DiBattista, D., 2006. Evidence that sensitivity to 6-n-propylthiouracil (PROP) affects perception of retro-nasal aroma intensity. *Journal of Food, Agriculture and Environment* 4, 15-22.
19 Feldman, R., Keren, M., Gross-Rozval, O., Tyano, S., 2004. Mother-Child touch patterns in infant feeding disorders: relation to maternal, child, and environmental factors. *Journal of the American Academy of Child and Adolescent Psychiatry*. 43(9), 1089-97.
20 Feldman, R., Rosenthal, Z., Eidelman, A.I., 2014. Maternal-preterm skin-to-skin contact enhances child physiologic organization and cognitive control across the first 10 years of life. *Biological Psychiatry* 75(1):56-64.
21 Kauer, J., Pelchat, M.L., Rozin, P., Zickgraf, H.F., 2015. Adult picky eating. Phenomenology, taste sensitivity, and psychological correlates. *Appetite* 90, 219-28.
22 Ibid., 10.
23 Nederkoorn, C., Jansen, A., Havermans, R.C., 2015. Feel your food. The influence of tactile sensitivity on picky eating in children. *Appetite* 84, 7-10.
24 Werthmann, J., Roefs, A., Havermans, R., Nederkoorn, C., Kremers, S., Jansen, A., 2014. Bits and pieces. Food texture influences food acceptance in young children. *Appetite* 84, 181-7.
25 See: Dazeley, P., Carmel Houston-Price, C., 2015. Exposure to foods' non-taste sensory properties. A nursery
intervention to increase children's willingness to try fruit and vegetables. *Appetite* 84, 1-6; Heath, P., Houston-Price, C., Kennedy, O.B., 2011. Increasing food familiarity without the tears. A role for visual exposure? *Appetite* 57(3), 832-8.

**Day 19**

1 Larsen, J.K., Hermans, R.C., Sleddens, E.F., Engels, R.C., Fisher, J.O., Kremers, S.P., 2015. How parental dietary behavior and food parenting practices affect children's dietary behavior. Interacting sources of influence?
*Appetite* 89, 246-57.
2 Jansen, E., Mallan, K.M., Nicholson, J.M., Daniels, L.A., 2014. The feeding practices and structure questionnaire: construction and initial validation in a sample of Australian first-time mothers and their 2-year olds. *International Journal of Behavioral Nutrition and Physical Activity* 11, 72.

3 Ibid., 1.
4 Ibid., 1.
5 Ibid., 1.
6 Ibid., 1.

**Day 20**

1 Trofholz, A.C., Schulte, A.K., Berge, J.M., 2017. How parents describe picky eating and its impact on family meals: a qualitative analysis. *Appetite* 110, 36-43.
2 Taylor, C.M., Northstone, K., Wernimont, S.M., Emmett, P.M., 2016. Macro- and micronutrient intakes in picky eaters: a cause for concern? *The American Journal of Clinical Nutrition* 104(6), 1647–1656.
3 Larsen, J.K., Hermans, R.C., Sleddens, E.F., Engels, R.C., Fisher, J.O., Kremers, S.P., 2015. How parental dietary behavior and food parenting practices affect children's dietary behavior. Interacting sources of influence? *Appetite* 89, 246-57.

**Day 21**

1 Satter, E., 2001. *Child of Mine: Feeding with Love and Good Sense.* 3rd sub edition. Boulder, CO: Bull Publishing Company.

**Day 22**

1 See for example: Kohn, A., 2018. *Unconditional Parenting: Moving from Rewards and Punishments to Love and Reason.* 1st trade paperback edition. New York: Atria Books.

**Day 23**

1 Tharner, A., Jansen, P.W., Kiefte-de Jong, J.C., Moll, H.A.,van der Ende, J., Jaddoe, V.W.V., Hofman, A., Tiemeier, H., Franco, O.H., 2014. Toward an operative diagnosis of fussy/picky eating: a latent profile approach in a population-based cohort. *International Journal of Behavioral Nutrition and Physical Activity* 11, 14.
2 Chong Cole, N., An, R., Lee, S-Y., Sharon M Donovan, S.M., 2017. Correlates of picky eating and food neophobia in young children: a systematic review and meta-analysis. *Nutrition Reviews* 75(7), 516–532.
3 Ünüsan, N., 2006. University students' food preference and practice now and during childhood. *Food Quality and Preference* 17(5), 362-368.

4 Larsen, J.K., Hermans, R.C., Sleddens, E.F., Engels, R.C., Fisher, J.O., Kremers, S.P., 2015. How parental dietary behavior and food parenting practices affect children's dietary behavior. Interacting sources of influence?
*Appetite* 89, 246-57.
5 Birch, L.L., 1999. Development of food preferences. *Annual Review of Nutrition* 19, 41-62.
6 Cooke, L.J., Chambers, L.C., Añez, E.V., Croker, H.A., Boniface, D., Yeomans, M.R., Wardle, J., 2011. Eating for pleasure or profit: the effect of incentives on children's enjoyment of vegetables. *Psychological Science* 22(2), 190–196.
7 Ibid., 3.
8 Birch, L. L., Zimmerman, S. I., Hind, H., 1980. The influence of social-affective context on the formation of children's food preferences. *Child Development* 51(3), 856-861; Birch, L.L., Birch, D., Marlin, D.W., Kramer, L., 1982. Effects of instrumental consumption on children's food preference. *Appetite* 3(2), 125-34; Birch, L.L., Marlin, D.W., Rotter, J., 1984. Eating as the "Means" Activity in a Contingency: Effects on Young Children's Food Preference. *Child Development* 55(2), 431-439.
9 Gibson, E. L., Kreichauf, S., Wildgruber, A., Vögele, C., Summerbell, C.D., Nixon, C., Moore, H., Douthwaite, W., Manios, Y., 2012. A narrative review of psychological and educational strategies applied to young children's eating behaviours aimed at reducing obesity risk. *Obesity Reviews* 13(Suppl. 1), 85–95.
10 Ibid., 3.

**Day 24**

1 Oliveria, S.A., Ellison, R.C., Moore, L.L., Gillman, M.W., Garrahie, E.J., Singer, M.R., 1992. Parent-child relationships in nutrient intake: the Framingham Children's Study. *The American Journal of Clinical Nutrition* 56(3), 593-8.
2 Ibid.
3 Larsen, J.K., Hermans, R.C., Sleddens, E.F., Engels, R.C., Fisher, J.O., Kremers, S.P., 2015. How parental dietary behavior and food parenting practices affect children's dietary behavior. Interacting sources of influence?
*Appetite* 89, 246-57.
4 Paroche, M.M., Caton, S.J., Vereijken, C.M.J.L., Weenen, H., Houston-Price, C., 2017. How Infants and Young Children Learn About Food: A Systematic Review. *Frontiers in Psychology* 25(8), 1046.
5 See: Horodynski, M.A., Stommel, M., Brophy-Herb, H., Xie, Y., Weatherspoon, L., 2010. Low-income African American and non-Hispanic White mothers' self-efficacy, "picky eater" perception, and toddler fruit and vegetable consumption. *Public Health Nursing* 27(5), 408-417; Cassells, E.L., Magarey, A.M., Daniels, L.A., Mallan, K.M.,

2014. The influence of maternal infant feeding practices and beliefs on the expression of food neophobia in toddlers. *Appetite* 82, 36-42.
6 Bruce, L.J., Ricciardelli, L.A., 2016. A systematic review of the psychosocial correlates of intuitive eating among adult women. *Appetite* 96, 454-472.
7 Escalona, S.K., 1945. Feeding disturbances in very young children. *American Journal of Orthopsychiatry 15*(1), 76-80.
8 Martins, Y., Pelchat, M.L., Pliner, P., 1997. "Try it; it's good and it's good for you": effects of taste and nutrition information on willingness to try novel foods. *Appetite* 28(2), 89-102.
9 Barthomeuf, L., Droit-Volet, S., Rousset, S., 2012. How emotions expressed by adults' faces affect the desire to eat liked and disliked foods in children compared to adults. *British Journal of Developmental Psychology* 30(2), 253-66.
10 Greenhalgh, J., Dowey, A.J., Horne, P., Lowe, C., Griffiths, J.H., Whitaker, C., 2009. Positive- and negative peer modelling effects on young children's consumption of novel blue foods. *Appetite* 52, 646-53.
11 Lafraire, J., Rioux, C., Giboreau, A., Picard, D., 2016. Food rejections in children: Cognitive and social/environmental factors involved in food neophobia and picky/fussy eating behavior. *Appetite* 96, 347-357.
12 Addessi, E., Galloway, A.T., Visalberghi, E., Birch, L.L., 2005. Specific social influences on the acceptance of novel foods in 2-5-year-old children. *Appetite* 45(3), 264-71.
13 Birch, L., 1980. Effects of peers models food choice and eating behavior on preschoolers food preferences. *Child Development* 51, 489-496.
14 Ibid., 7.
15 Wadhera, D., Capaldi Phillips, E.D., Wilkie, L.M.. 2015. Teaching children to like and eat vegetables. *Appetite* 93, 75-84.

**Day 25**

1 Kohn, A., 2018. *Unconditional Parenting: Moving from Rewards and Punishments to Love and Reason.* 1st trade paperback edition. New York: Atria Books.
2 See for example: Chatoor, I., Egan, J., Getson, P., Menvielle, E., O'donnell, R., 1988. Mother—Infant Interactions in Infantile Anorexia Nervosa. *Journal of the American Academy of Child & Adolescent Psychiatry* 27(5), 535–540.
3 Satter, E., 2001. *Child of Mine: Feeding with Love and Good Sense.* 3rd sub edition. Boulder, CO: Bull Publishing Company, p.373.
4 For some children with sensory processing issues, an Occupational Therapist or other qualified practitioner may advise on ways of stimulating or reducing the sensory information that your child receives at mealtimes, which may include distractions.
5 van der Horst, K., 2012. Overcoming picky eating. Eating enjoyment as a central aspect of children's eating behaviors. *Appetite* 58(2), 567-74.

**Day 26**

1 Infant and Toddler Forum, 2016. *#rethinktoddlerportionsizes* [online]. Available from: https://www.infantandtoddlerforum.org/media/upload/pdf-downloads/ITF-portion-sizes-survey.pdf [Accessed 5th April 2019].

2 Rolls, B.J., Engell, D., Birch, L.L., 2000. Serving portion size influences 5-year-old but not 3-year-old children's food intakes. *The Journal of the American Dietetic Association* 100(2), 232-4.

3 Powell, F., Farrow, C., Haycraft, E., Meyer, C., 2011. Appetite regulation in early childhood: the impact of parenting behaviours and child temperament. *In*: Mitchell, S.R. (ed.) *Appetite: Regulation, Role in Disease and Control.* Hauppauge NY: Nova Science Publishers, 1-28.

4 Gibson, A.A., Hsu, M.S., Rangan, A.M., Seimon, R.V., Lee, C.M., Das, A., Finch, C.H., Sainsbury, A., 2016. Accuracy of hands v. household measures as portion size estimation aids. *Journal of Nutrition Science* 5, e29.

5 Infant and Toddler Forum. Available from: https://www.infantandtoddlerforum.org/portion-sizes-table-2015 [Accessed 5th April 2019].

**Day 27**

1 Fraker, C., Fishbein, M., Cox, S., Walbert, L., 2007. Food Chaining: The Proven 6-Step Plan to Stop Picky Eating, Solve Feeding Problems, and Expand Your Child's Diet. Boston, Massachusetts: Da Capo Press.

2 Fisher, J.O., Mennella, J.A., Hughes, S.O., Liu, Y., Mendoza, P.M., Patrick, H., 2012. Offering "Dip" Promotes Intake of a Moderately-Liked Raw Vegetable among Preschoolers with Genetic Sensitivity to Bitterness. *Journal of the Academy of Nutrition and Dietetics* 112(2), 235-45.

**Day 28**

1 Harris, G., Mason, S., 2017. Are There Sensitive Periods for Food Acceptance in Infancy? *Current Nutrition Reports* 6(2), 190–196.

2 Manno, C.J., Fox, C., Eicher, P.S., Kerwin, M.L.E., 2005. Early oral-motor interventions for pediatric feeding problems: what, when and how. *Journal of Early and Intensive Behavior Intervention* 2(3), 145.

3 Benoit, D., Wang, E.E.L., Zlotkin, S.H., 2000. Discontinuation of enterostomy tube feeding by behavioral treatment in early childhood: A randomized controlled trial. *The Journal of Pediatrics* 137(4), 498–503.

4 For a discussion on the topic, see: Jones, C.J. and Bryant-Waugh, R., 2013. The relationship between child-feeding problems and maternal mental health: a selective review. *Advances in Eating Disorders: Theory, Research and Practice*, 1(2), 119-133.
5 Pridham, K.F., Schroeder, M., Brown, R., Clark, R., 2001. The relationship of a mother's working model of feeding to her feeding behaviour. *Journal of Advanced Nursing* 35(5), 741-750.
6 Harris, G., Booth, I.W., 2006. The nature and management of eating problems in pre-school children. *In*: Cooper, P.J., Stein, A. eds. *Childhood feeding problems and adolescent eating disorders*. Abingdon-on-Thames: Routledge.
7 Ibid., 5.
8 Rommel, N., De Meyer, A.M., Feenstra, L., Veereman-Wauters, G., 2003. The complexity of feeding problems in 700 infants and young children presenting to a tertiary care institution. *Journal of Pediatric Gastroenterology and Nutrition* 37(1), 75-84.
9 Mason, S.J., Harris, G., Blissett, J., 2005. Tube feeding in infancy: implications for the development of normal eating and drinking skills. *Dysphagia* 20 (1), 46-61.
10 Krom, H., de Winter, P.J., Kindermann, A., 2017. Development, prevention, and treatment of feeding tube dependency. *European Journal of Pediatrics* 176(6), 683–688.
11 For a discussion on food reinforcement see for example: Epstein, L. H., Leddy, J.J., Temple, J.L., Faith, M.S., 2007. Food Reinforcement and Eating: A Multilevel Analysis. *Psychological Bulletin* 133(5), 884–906.
12 Bhattacharyya, N., 2015. The prevalence of pediatric voice and swallowing problems in the United States. *Laryngoscope* 125(3), 746-50.
13 Arvedson, J.C., 2008. Assessment of pediatric dysphagia and feeding disorders: clinical and instrumental approaches. *Developmental Disabilities Research Reviews* 14(2), 118-27.
14 Hendricks, K., Briefel, R., Novak, T., Ziegler, P., 2006. Maternal and child characteristics associated with infant and toddler feeding practices. .*Journal of the American Dietetic Association* 2006 Jan;106(1 Suppl 1):S135-48.
15 Maslin, K., Dean, T., Arshad, S.H., Venter, C., 2015. Fussy eating and feeding difficulties in infants and toddlers consuming a cows' milk exclusion diet. *Pediatric Allergy and Immunology* 26(6), 503-508.
16 Johnson, R., Harris, G., 2004. A preliminary study of the predictors of feeding problems in late infancy. *Journal of Reproductive and Infant Psychology* 22(3), 183-188.

**Day 29**

1 The National Institute of Health and Care Excellence (NICE), 2010. *Constipation in children and young people: diagnosis and management.* London: NICE. NICE Clinical guideline [CG99].
2 Tharner, A., Jansen, P.W., Kiefte-de Jong, J.C., Moll, H.A., Hofman, A., Jaddoe, V.W., Tiemeier, H., Franco, O.H. Bidirectional associations between fussy eating and functional constipation in preschool children. *The Journal of Pediatrics* 166(1), 91-6.
3 Manno, C.J., Fox, C., Eicher, P.S., Kerwin, M.L.E., 2005. Early oral-motor interventions for pediatric feeding problems: what, when and how. *Journal of Early and Intensive Behavior Intervention* 2(3), 145.
4 Ibid., 1.
5 Field, D., Garland, M., Williams, K., 2003. Correlates of specific childhood feeding problems. *Journal of Paediatrics and Child Health* 39(4), 299-304.
6 The National Institute of Health and Care Excellence (NICE), 2015. *Gastro-oesophageal reflux disease in children and young people: diagnosis and management.* London: NICE. NICE guideline [NG1].
7 The National Institute of Health and Care Excellence (NICE), 2011. *Food allergy in under 19s: assessment and diagnosis.* London: NICE. Clinical guideline [CG116].

Printed in Great Britain
by Amazon

85867237R00165